THE LITTLE BOOK OF
PEMBROKESHIRE

DR RUSSELL GRIGG

T0341943

The History Press

First published 2023

The History Press
97 St George's Place, Cheltenham,
Gloucestershire, GL50 3QB
www.thehistorypress.co.uk

British Library Cataloguing in Publication Data.
A catalogue record for this book is available from the British Library.

ISBN 978 0 7509 9950 2

Typesetting and origination by The History Press
Printed and bound in Great Britain by TJ Books Limited, Padstow, Cornwall.

Trees for Life

CONTENTS

ACKNOWLEDGEMENTS

Pembrokeshire has produced many fine historians since the sixteenth-century days of George Owen. Although this is a little book, it is indebted to their scholarship. For brevity, I have not included full references and sources, but have highlighted main contributions in the text and select bibliography. I am grateful to Tim Burton and Dr Sioned Hughes, friends and former colleagues, both of whom took time to read through the manuscript and offer helpful suggestions, drawing on their considerable local knowledge. I would like to thank Cadw for providing Figures 4 and 5. Thanks also to Juanita Hall and the team at The History Press for their support through the production process. And finally, thanks to Helen for her continued support and companionship during forays into Pembrokeshire, my home county.

LIST OF FIGURES

Fig. 1 Pembrokeshire, 1805. (*Piccadilly*, A Map of South Wales, *1805*)

INTRODUCTION

Pembrokeshire is a land of contrasts, which I know from personal experience. Although I was born and raised in the seaside resort of Tenby, I spent many weekends in my grandparents' cottage at Pontnewydd, on the banks of the River Nevern in north Pembrokeshire. Its charming, chocolate-box façade belied the absence of modern amenities. For example, the single toilet was at the end of the garden by the river, the bedrooms lacked central heating, and we often had to rely on candlelight due to power outages. Looking back, it's difficult to believe this was the 1960s and not the 1860s.

My maternal grandfather was a Welsh speaker, who learnt English by talking with summer visitors who stayed in the caravan park at Llwyngwair Manor, where my great grandfather worked as the lodge keeper. On my Tenby-based paternal side, no one spoke Welsh.

The binary nature of my own Pembrokeshire childhood is indicative of the county's deeper contrasts. For more than 900 years, the Welsh-speaking north and the anglicised south have been separated by an invisible frontier or boundary known as the *Landsker*; literally meaning a 'cut into the landscape'. Following the Norman Conquest of 1066, the Normans built a series of castles to keep the Welsh at bay. These stretch from Laugharne, on the Carmarthenshire coast, through Narberth, Wiston and Roch, approaching St Bride's Bay to the west. Place names are an indicator of this division, with the likes of Johnston and Honeyborough to the south and Eglwyswrw and Mynachlog-ddu to the north. The latter are within the district most strongly associated with the Welsh language (*Y Fro Gymraeg*), extending westwards from Anglesey through Ceredigion, Carmarthenshire and north Pembrokeshire. Modern DNA evidence confirms that the genetic make-up of those living in the north of the county differs from 'the down belows', who occupy what has been called for centuries 'Little England beyond Wales'.

The linguistic divide has been a sharp one. For example, in 1921, 97 per cent of those living in the parish of Llandeloy spoke Welsh, whereas less than 10 km away, in the parish of Nolton, the figure was only 3 per cent. However, the division has become less clear cut, with growing interest in Welsh language education in the south alongside migration and Anglicisation in the north. Moreover, the very notion of the *Landsker* for some has become outdated, with its emphasis on differences and the implication that those below the *Landsker* are 'less Welsh' than those to the north.

For thousands of first-language Welsh speakers like my grandfather, speaking Welsh is integral to their identity and everyday life, just as speaking French is in France. For the language to thrive, it needs local and national support. This has increased significantly since 1997, when Wales received devolved powers in areas such as education, which has added political impetus for Welsh-medium schooling in Anglicised towns such as Tenby, Haverfordwest and Pembroke. More than 40 per cent of educational provision in the county has some form of Welsh-medium teaching.

Language is an important but not defining characteristic of identity. Around 70 per cent of Pembrokeshire's population do not speak Welsh, according to the Welsh Government's population survey in 2021.

The question of identity is not simply an academic discussion. In 2022, when a frozen food company in Pembroke Dock advertised its ice cream as 'Made for you in Little England beyond Wales', it upset a lot of local people. The company duly apologised and changed its branding.

While there are differences among the communities of Pembrokeshire, perhaps they have more in common than sets them apart. For example, Pembrokeshire is united by its strong maritime tradition. There is also a shared sense of pride in the Pembrokeshire Coast National Park, designated in 1952, which embraces just over a third of the county. It is rightly considered by the Welsh Government as a major health and well-being resource, offering active benefits associated with the likes of surfing, sailing, diving, climbing, swimming, kayaking, coasteering, geocaching (a form of hide-and-seek), horse riding, caving, walking and cycling, and the passive joy of taking time out to absorb the likes of the ancient Pengelli Wood (near Eglwyswrw), which is at least 10,000 years old, or observing close up the puffins and other wildlife on Skomer Island.

The Pembrokeshire landscape is an evocative one that transcends the immediate senses. This experience was captured 1,000 years ago in *The Mabinogi*, the eleventh-century Welsh folktales which described Pembrokeshire as a land of mystery and enchantment (*Gwlad hud a lledrith*). The ancient hills and coast radiate magic in various forms, from myths and legends to the distinctive, reflective light, which have inspired generations of poets, writers, artists, musicians, mystics and others.

It continues to do so. Pembrokeshire beaches have featured in films such as *Harry Potter and the Deathly Hallows* (2009), Ridley Scott's *Robin Hood* (2010) and *Snow White and the Huntsman* (2012). As the recent pandemic restrictions eased, one journalist visiting from London commented that Pembrokeshire was 'untamed, underrated and ripe for adventure'.

In fact, Pembrokeshire has long been valued as a special place. Perhaps it is because of its size – little more than 30 miles as the crow flies, north to south or east to west (Figure 2). 'There is no spot where the peasantry exhibit more happiness than in the northern parts of Pembrokeshire,' wrote one travel writer in 1799, while a modern guidebook confidently proclaims, 'Pembrokeshire possesses everything'.

Many residents have gone so far as to suggest that this is 'God's own country'. The fact that this has also been said of places as far apart as New Zealand, India and Zimbabwe, or closer to home, Yorkshire, does not seem to matter. Pembrokeshire is held up as offering something for everyone – from ramblers, nature lovers and surfers, to musicians, artists, filmmakers and poets, from those looking for a barmy summer stag or hen party in Tenby to those seeking monastic solitude on Caldey Island or spiritual renewal in St Davids Cathedral.

As this book aims to highlight, Pembrokeshire has much to offer in its rich heritage, culture and breathtaking coastline, widely regarded as the best in the world. It also has a fascinating history and I have tried to bring this to life with human stories about work, poverty, health, travel, war, education, entertainment and other themes that have affected people's lives in Pembrokeshire.

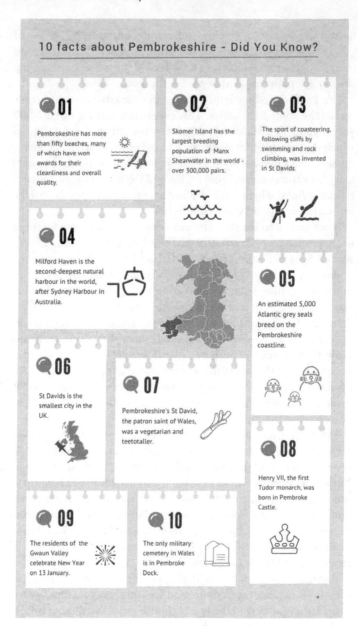

10 facts about Pembrokeshire - Did You Know?

01 Pembrokeshire has more than fifty beaches, many of which have won awards for their cleanliness and overall quality.

02 Skomer Island has the largest breeding population of Manx Shearwater in the world - over 300,000 pairs.

03 The sport of coasteering, following cliffs by swimming and rock climbing, was invented in St Davids.

04 Milford Haven is the second-deepest natural harbour in the world, after Sydney Harbour in Australia.

05 An estimated 5,000 Atlantic grey seals breed on the Pembrokeshire coastline.

06 St Davids is the smallest city in the UK.

07 Pembrokeshire's St David, the patron saint of Wales, was a vegetarian and teetotaller.

08 Henry VII, the first Tudor monarch, was born in Pembroke Castle.

09 The residents of the Gwaun Valley celebrate New Year on 13 January.

10 The only military cemetery in Wales is in Pembroke Dock.

Fig. 2 Pembrokeshire – Did You Know?

1

BEGINNINGS

When does Pembrokeshire (*Sir Benfro*) begin? The name itself means 'headland' and is a combination of the old Brythonic or Welsh words, *Pen* (head) and *Bro* (region or district). Originally, *Penfro* was one of the land divisions or *cantrefs* which made up the old medieval kingdom of Dyfed. The shire element in Pembrokeshire comes from the Anglo-Saxon '*scir*', a model of local government based on the 'shire-reeves', or sheriffs, who were responsible for keeping order and collecting taxes on behalf of the king.

With the arrival of the Normans, Pembroke was made a county palatine in 1138, which meant that the Earl of Pembroke was granted special authority on behalf of the king. But it was not until the reforms of Henry VIII that the territory of modern Pembrokeshire began to take shape. Through the Acts of Union (1536 and 1542–43), Wales was divided into thirteen Welsh counties or shires, where the same English laws were to apply. In 1974, these were reorganised into eight new counties, one of which was Dyfed, comprising Pembrokeshire, Carmarthenshire and Cardiganshire. While the name Dyfed remains in use for certain purposes, such as policing (Dyfed-Powys Police), as a term for council administration it proved unpopular. Hence, in 1996 the old counties of Pembrokeshire, Cardiganshire (which became Ceredigion) and Carmarthenshire were reinstated.

Natural history affords another perspective on how the area has developed. As the writer Vyvyan Rees put it, 'Stones, the sea and the weather have moulded the look of Pembrokeshire. Man has merely scratched the service.'

In terms of geology, Pembrokeshire began in the age of volcanic activity when Precambrian rocks formed St Davids Peninsula, around 650 million years ago. Over a very long period of time, a series of severe climate changes with variations between glacial (cold) and interglacial (warm) years created different landscapes, climates, fauna and environments. The legacy can be seen in northern Pembrokeshire, where valleys were carved out and the rugged hills of igneous rock and slate were splintered by the Irish Sea glaciations.

At one time the sea level around the Welsh coastline was estimated to be at least 50m below the present level because so much water was locked up in ice. During the last glaciation, about 18,500 years ago, ice probably enclosed the whole of Pembrokeshire. The Irish Sea Ice Sheet covered St Davids Peninsula, reaching the Preseli Hills to the north and as far south as the entrance to Milford Haven. As the climate warmed up, sea levels rose and the islands of Ramsey, Skomer and Skokholm were eventually cut off from the mainland.

Pembrokeshire has been left with a range of impressive geological features, including:

- The Three Chimneys on Marloes Sands – near-vertical sandstones that stand out in the cliff
- Red Berry Bay on Caldey Island, named after the red sandstone cliffs
- Den's Door, north of Broadhaven, one of two sea arches
- the Ladies' Cave anticline at Saundersfoot – a remarkable chevron fold
- the Green Bridge of Wales, Castlemartin – covered in vegetation and formed in the age of the dinosaurs
- Pen-y-holt Stack, Castlemartin – a limestone sea stack
- Huntsman's Leap, south of Bosherston – a deep limestone chasm
- columnar ballast at Pen Anglas headland, showing pillow-shaped lavas.

Around 40 per cent of the Pembrokeshire coastline comprises geological features that are protected as Sites of Special Scientific Interest (SSSI). This means that they represent the best of our natural heritage, whether rocks, landform, flora or fauna. The coastline itself is regarded as one of the most stunning in the UK, if not the world. Its extraordinary range of rock colours and textures has left many sightseers in awe. As the writer Brian John explains, 'One minute you are walking along the top of a high vertical cliff, and one minute later you are on the lee side of a headland where a low sloping cliff is covered by luxuriant vegetation.'

The moist, warm oceanic climate, along with the variations in rock and soil, support a wide range of habitats for plants and wildlife. The grasslands and heath on the more exposed coastal slopes and clifftops contrast with sand dunes in broad bays, freshwater marshes and fens in coastal river valleys. Pembrokeshire's mild climate and its fertile soil offer a long growing season, notably for early potatoes. In 2013, the European Commission awarded Pembrokeshire Earlies Protected Geographical Indication status (PGI), meaning they have the same protection as Champagne and Parma ham.

* * *

While geology tells us how Pembrokeshire was formed over millennia, when does the human story in this region begin?

Archaeologists estimate that the earliest bones in Wales date to around 225,000 BC and were discovered in Pontnewydd Cave (Denbighshire). These were the remains of Neanderthals, considered an archaic species of humans, named after their discovery in Germany's Neander Valley. The bones of bear, horse, deer and hyena along with flint tools have been found at Hoyle's Mouth (Penally), dated to around 30,000 years ago.

Until the nineteenth century, it was commonly thought that human origins could be traced back to no more than 6,000 years ago, but the emergence of archaeology as a science showed that humans have a much older existence. When in 1851 stone axes were discovered in Devon alongside the remains of cave bears, woolly rhinoceros and other extinct species (all under a sealed rock), a new term was invented to describe the vast age before writing was invented: 'prehistoric'.

PREHISTORY

If the time when humans are known to have lived in Britain is visualised as a 100 squares, 99.9 of those squares would be occupied by prehistory. The chronology of prehistory is typically split into ages based on how soon the earliest peoples mastered various technologies. The Stone Age, the first of these ages, is so vast that archaeologists further subdivide this into three phases so that they can more accurately describe changes over time.

The Old Stone Age, or Palaeolithic (c.225,000–8000 BC)

The most significant development in the Old Stone Age was the mastery of fire, which is seen as a mark of human intelligence which separated us from animals. Fire provided warmth and lighting, protection from predators, a means for cooking, forging spears, axes, beads and bows, and a social focus, which indirectly helped develop language.

Fire was essential in surviving the freezer of ice-age winters. During the most recent glaciation (about 18,500 years ago), the northern part of Pembrokeshire remained covered in ice, but the south was exposed and experienced tundra conditions. The melting of the ice drowned river valleys, creating the likes of the Milford Haven waterway. The dramatic shingle ridge at Newgale beach is a legacy of the last glaciation and is the longest beach in the county (2.5km or 2 miles, end to end). The ice also carried boulders (known as erratics, after the Latin word '*errare*', meaning to wander) hundreds of kilometres from their original location. One interesting aside is that two of these boulders formed the headstones for the burials of Colonel Francis Lambton and his wife, Lady Victoria, from Castlemartin. They were amateur geologists who, in the early 1900s, restored the medieval Flimston Chapel, which sits in the middle of the Castlemartin Royal Armoured Corps firing range, and has done since 1940.

Marine archaeologists have mapped how prehistoric Pembrokeshire changed, using survey data of the seabed. Towards the end of the Palaeolithic period, around 10,000 years ago, Britain was still joined by a 'land bridge' to mainland Europe, while Cardigan Bay, Liverpool Bay, the Severn Estuary and the Bristol Channel simply did not exist.

The Middle Stone Age, or Mesolithic (c.8000–4500 BC)

For archaeologists, Nab Head in Pembrokeshire is the most significant Mesolithic site. Climate changes meant that the original site would have been around 6km inland from its present coastal edge. It has been likened to a kind of production factory for making tools and processing food. Incredibly, more than 40,000 stone tools and 700 stone discs or beads have been discovered here over the course of a series of excavations conducted since the nineteenth century. The beads are a couple of millimetres thick and with a single hole drilled from one side, resembling polo mints. They were probably used as a medium of trade.

Another remarkable Mesolithic discovery was made in 2010 when a Lydstep resident contacted Dyfed Archaeological Trust to report unusual footprints on the beach. They had been solidified in a peat deposit that was once the floor of a shallow lagoon in the late Mesolithic period. The deep impression suggests that a group of adults and children were standing still, waiting for some time in one place. Archaeologists speculate that this was a hunting party, hidden in the reeds, ready to pounce on any unsuspecting animal about to take a drink.

The footprints were close, and possibly linked, to an earlier discovery known as the Lydstep Pig. In 1917, local antiquarian Arthur Leach found a wild boar skeleton trapped beneath a tree trunk with two broken flint points in its neck. The Lydstep Pig is estimated to be 6,300 years old. While the hunters may have caught their prey for food, it is also possible that the pig was a votive offering at the water's edge, pinned down by a tree trunk. Water, with its cleansing and life-giving qualities, has long been associated with rituals. It is remarkable how a child of our time can walk along the beach and place her feet in the prints of a young Mesolithic hunter – one small step in a connection spanning thousands of years.

Another important discovery followed the winter storms of 2013–14. Remnants of Mesolithic trees and human footprints along Newgale beach were exposed as high seas swept aside a bank of pebbles which had covered them. This woodland area may have been the site of hunters and gatherers searching for game and edible plants, nuts and berries 10,000 years ago. Following the storm, a Newgale resident found the horns of an auroch, an ancestor of our domestic cattle, which became extinct in the seventeenth century. Perhaps this was the prey of the prehistoric hunting party.

As yet, no Mesolithic houses have been found in Pembrokeshire, unlike in other parts of the UK, such as Star Carr in Yorkshire. The traditional view is that hunter-gatherers did not have fixed settlements but moved around, depending upon the seasonal search for food. They gathered wild plants, hunted animals, birds and fish, and used animal skins to make clothes. They may have lived in caves or used temporary shelters as they travelled.

The remains of Mesolithic reindeer and woolly mammoth bones have been discovered in Wogan Cavern under Pembroke Castle. In 2021, while the wardens on Skokholm Island were in lockdown due to the coronavirus, they discovered a 'bevelled pebble' in a rabbit's hole. Archaeologists later confirmed that this was a prehistoric tool, probably used by hunter-gatherers to shape seal hides for use as skin-covered vessels or for processing shellfish.

The New Stone Age, or Neolithic (c.4500–2500 BC)

The New Stone Age is marked by a gradual decline in hunter-gathering, with the introduction of domesticated animals, the clearance of woodland, the beginnings of arable farming and the emergence of settlements. In 2021, archaeologists found dairy fat residue, probably from yoghurt, in shards of decorated pottery at Trellyffaint, near Newport. This suggests that dairy farming in Pembrokeshire has been practised for at least 5,000 years, the earliest proof of dairy farming in Wales. The remains of timber and daub huts with stone footings at Clegyr Boia near St Davids (Figure 3) and Rhos y Clegyrn, point to the existence of small farming groups growing wheat and barley and keeping cattle, pigs and sheep.

Technological developments included the use of polished stone axes. These were made by chipping a flint block into a rudimentary

Fig. 3 Farming settlement around 4000 BC by Giovanni Caselli, 1979. Based on excavations at Clegyr Boia, St Davids, Pembrokeshire, in 1902 and 1943. (©Amgueddfa Cymru – Museum Wales)

shape before grinding and polishing it with sand and water. Experiments show that these polished axes can be as effective as modern steel ones when applied to birch and other softwood. The Preseli Hills provided the raw material to make these axes.

Communities started to build megalithic structures, which served several purposes. Primarily, they were sites for communal burials, often over many generations. It is possible that these were focal points for social gatherings.

Pembrokeshire has around eighty known burial places. The most impressive and iconic of the monuments is Pentre Ifan (at Nevern), which is older than the Egyptian pyramids. The raised stone weighs 16 tons and the structure dates to around 6,000 years ago. When Victorian tourists visited in 1859, five persons on horseback were reportedly capable of standing beneath the capstone at the same time. The Victorians thought that it served as a resting place for a local chieftain and his family. They also concluded that the build-ers moved the stones into place from the ridge nearby using some 'rude mechanical appliances'. The initial act of moving and raising such large stones likely involved a combination of brute force and wooden rollers and ropes (Figures 4 and 5).

Pentre Ifan is one of many ancient monuments and burial sites to be found within the Newport–Nevern district. Some of these are on private property and can only be accessed by foot. Carreg Coetan Arthur, on the banks of the River Nevern, is one of the best preserved. King Arthur is supposed to have played a game of quoits ('*coetan*') with the stone of the tomb, where cremated human remains and stone tools have been found. The Carreg Samson dolmen (at Abercastle), which overlooks Cardigan Bay, has a capstone which weighs around 25 tons resting on three uprights. It has been estimated that to erect the whole structure would have taken up to 15,000 worker-hours. But the biggest cap-stone in Britain is to be found at Garne Turne (near Wolfscastle), which is estimated to weigh 80 tons, the equivalent of 100 cows.

Of Pembrokeshire's ancient stone circles, the most striking is at Gors Fawr (near Mynachlog-ddu), about 22m across, comprising an almost perfect ring of sixteen pillars or boulders. Two other notable monuments are Bedd Arthur (technically an oval setting rather than a circle), comprising seventeen bluestones at the east

Figs 4 & 5 Modern interpretation of how stones may have been moved to create Pentre Ifan. (*Cadw, illustration by Jane Durrant,* © Crown, 2022)

end of the Preseli ridge, and Carn Menyn Cairn (near Mynachlog-ddu). In total, around seventy or so standing stones exist, serving as uprights of burial chambers or forming free-standing monuments, as funeral memorials, objects of worship, boundary markers or commemorations of events, such as battles.

THE BLUESTONE MYSTERY OF STONEHENGE

Archaeologists have long debated how stones weighing up to 4 tons from the Preseli Hills in Pembrokeshire found their way to Stonehenge, in Wiltshire, a distance of 150 miles (250km). One theory is that they were moved on sledges and rollers to Milford Haven, from there on rafts across the Bristol Channel, up the River Avon and then again on sledges and rollers to their final destination. Perhaps horsepower was involved at some stage. Another theory is that the monoliths were moved much earlier in time, perhaps half a million years ago, by shifting glaciers.

Recent analysis of charcoal and sedimentary remains at Waun Mawn in the Preseli Hills suggests that an original circle of blue-stones may have been dismantled and relocated to Stonehenge as the Preseli people migrated, perhaps as a reminder of their ancestral identity. Archaeologists estimate that Waun Mawn once had a circle of between thirty and fifty stones, but only four remain there.

The archaeologist Francis Pryor reminds us that we should not think of Stonehenge in modern terms, as some form of civic engineering project governed by efficiency and effectiveness. Rather, he speculates that the actual transportation and erection of the stones formed part of a ceremonial ritual, a joyous event with feasting, singing and socialising in the evenings. Perhaps the act of moving the bluestones was a symbolic means of unifying two different ancestries from different parts of Britain.

An examination of the stones has shown that they even have musical qualities. When tapped with a small 'hammer', the stones emit a ringing quality.

There are also suggestions that the stones had religious significance or medicinal qualities when seen in relation to water. The original Stonehenge site had an Avenue which connected the stones to the River Avon. One view is that the Pembrokeshire bluestones formed a temple and were seen to possess curative powers, offering comfort and protection to pilgrims and travellers drawn to the area.

We do not know exactly how and why the bluestones came to be at Stonehenge, but this is among Pembrokeshire's best-known contribution to British heritage.

The Bronze Age (c.2500–600 BC)

The landscape of Pembrokeshire and the rest of Wales was transformed by the discovery of metals, which led to the development of the plough and the wheel. The earliest metalworkers in Britain used copper, gold and bronze to forge axes, daggers and other weapons, as well as ornaments. In Wales, the earliest records of metal tools date to about 4,000 years ago. The most significant findings in Pembrokeshire include a hoard of spearheads from a peat bog in Freshwater West in 1991 and various objects found at Marloes in 2013, including fragments of two sword blades, a scabbard fitting, a knife and six pieces of copper ingot. Although gold was mined at Dolaucothi (Carmarthenshire) from at least 5,000 years ago, the only item of gold found in Pembrokeshire to date is a crumpled gold 'lock-ring' from Newport, now held by the National Museum of Wales and viewable online.[1]

During the Bronze Age the importance of megaliths declined, with tombs being blocked and abandoned. Round barrows and cairns started to appear, and new styles of Beaker pottery and the working of flint were increasingly adopted. It is estimated that Pembrokeshire has around 160 round barrows of up to 4,000 in the whole of Wales. They vary in shape and size, reflecting the status of the individuals buried. The largest and most famous are the three stone cairns on the summit of

1   https://museum.wales/collections/bronze-age-gold-from-wales/object/
    eb9e3f9c-cce7-39de-a8f3-7df923819924/Late-Bronze-Age-gold-lock-
    ring/content/

Foel Drygarn, each around 25m in diameter and standing 3m high. This may have covered the bones or ashes of high-ranking individuals. These burial cairns were never plundered for their stone, despite being surrounded by hundreds of shelters within the settlement, which suggests that there was a high degree of reverence for dead ancestors.

The presence of stray finds and scattered monuments shows that people were active right across Pembrokeshire in the late Bronze Age. In 2006, archaeologists revealed numerous Bronze Age cremations at Steynton (Milford Haven) while the new South Wales Gas Pipeline was being laid. More than twenty adults and children were buried at the site, along with food vessels and urns for the next life. Archaeologists have also found evidence of pits, hearths, troughs and burnt stone, the remnants of a cooking place where water was once heated.

The standing stone at Devil's Quoit, Stackpole Warren, is 1.7m tall and likely formed part of a timber structure that burnt down around 3,400 years ago. It is perhaps a site of ritual and domestic significance, being the earliest date for such a Bronze Age structure. Archaeologists who excavated the surrounding field system found nearly 800 flints, along with evidence of roundhouses, cooking pits, hearths, charred cereal grains and pottery sherds, suggesting the area was inhabited over many centuries, spanning the Neolithic to Roman periods.

It was once thought that waves of immigrants from central Europe arrived in Britain, bringing a new 'Celtic' culture and language by about 600 BC. Archaeologists now emphasise continuity rather than sudden change and the merging of cultures through trade, marriage, feasting and festivals. Rather than acting as barriers, the western seaways were important channels of communication and exchange between Pembrokeshire, north-west Wales, south-west England and Brittany. The presence of hilltop enclosures, the appearance of iron and the development of tools and weaponry were signs of new ways of life that would come to characterise the next phase of human settlement.

2

THE IRON AGE CELTS, *c.*600 BC–AD 48

The oldest surviving written references to what is now Wales and Pembrokeshire appeared in the second century AD when the Greek cartographer Claudius Ptolemy mentioned the *Demetae*, the Celtic tribe, whom the Romans say occupied south-west Wales. We know hardly anything about these people, although more generally the Classical writers regarded the '*Keltoi*' or '*Celtae*' as ignorant, uncivilised 'barbarians' who babbled, making unintelligible sounds ('bar bar bar'). Unfortunately, we do not know what the Celts thought because they left no written records. Their culture emphasised storytelling, metal and craftwork rather than reading and writing.

The Celts may have lived up to their reputation for being 'madly fond of war, high-spirited and quick to battle'. But they were also highly skilled craftsmen, evidenced by surviving brooches, cauldrons, decorative pins, shields and swords, which are exhibited in the National Museum of Wales, the British Museum and museums across Europe. Goldsmiths produced stunning torcs, or necklaces, which provided the wearer with divine protection and a sense of mystery, wealth and status.

The Celts were also excellent horsemen and charioteers, masters of wheeled vehicles. In 2018, a local metal detectorist found an Iron Age chariot burial in an undisclosed field in south Pembrokeshire, the first of its kind in Wales. It not only transformed his life, with reports of him receiving a six-figure treasure payment, but it also enhanced our understanding of how such technology and burial practices spread – all of the other British chariot burials found thus far have been unearthed in northern England, notably Yorkshire. The likelihood is that the chariot was owned by a local tribal chief.

The Celts are famous for their hillforts, which offered protection for farms and a place to store food, while also acting as a centre for social activities. There is evidence for around 600 hillforts in Wales, more than 100 of which are found in Pembrokeshire. Most of these were probably small in scale, supporting a family or two. Carn Alw, on the western side of the Preseli Hills, served as a small, enclosed space, possibly a summer grazing retreat or refuge. In contrast, Foel Drygarn ('hill of three cairns'), on the top of the Preseli Hills, covered several hectares and was likely a tribal headquarters accommodating a couple of hundred people.

The large stone hillfort on Carn Ingli, with its array of ramparts, enclosures and huts, was first mentioned in the twelfth century as the site where St Brynach reputedly communed with angels. But far more common than this were smaller hillforts defended by banks and ditches and limited to less than 1 hectare. Promontory forts jutted out and incorporated steep cliffs as part of their natural defences. Around 100 or so of these have been identified, such as Dale Fort and Porth y Rhaw.

Hillforts were built for shelter and protection. Among the various defensive features of the larger hillforts was the *cheval de frise*, consisting of upright stones placed in a band outside the main defences with the aim of halting or slowing down the enemy's advancing chariots. Excavations at the partially reconstructed Iron Age settlement at Castell Henllys ('Old Palace'), near Eglwyswrw, show that its *cheval de frise* was preserved under a later defensive bank, suggesting that it was only meant as a temporary measure to be covered over once more substantial resources were available for defence. Several thousand slingstones have been found at Castell Henllys. These were an effective weapon in ancient times, highlighted in the biblical story of David slaying Goliath. An experienced slinger could kill or inflict a serious injury at a distance of 60m or more.

Castell Henllys provides modern-day visitors with a sense of what life might have been like 2,000 years ago, living among the *Demetae*. Unusually for a promontory fort, the high ground is at the bottom of the site, while the surrounding defences are hidden in trees. The site is approached through leafy woodland and ascends to an open area of just over an acre. This is small in comparison to other Iron Age settlements. Maiden Castle (Dorset), for example, covers 47 acres.

Castell Henllys contains four roundhouses and a granary, which have been carefully reconstructed on the original Iron Age foundation postholes. Two of the four roundhouses have in recent years been dismantled, re-excavated and reconstructed. One of the roundhouse roofs has been rethatched twice.

Archaeologists have been working on the site for nearly forty years. They calculate that the construction of the largest round-house alone required thirty coppiced oak trees, ninety coppiced hazel bushes, 2,000 bundles of water reeds and 2 miles of hemp rope and twine, necessary for forming its rafters, posts, ring-beams and wattle walls.

The process of gathering, assembling and maintaining these materials required huge amounts of effort, teamwork and deter-mination. Archaeologists estimate that approximately 100 people lived and worked in a self-supporting community, producing their own food, clothes, equipment, tools and weapons. The site was occupied from the fifth to the second or first century BC.

For some unknown reason, Castell Henllys was abandoned in the late Iron Age. The site may have been occupied in later centuries by Irish settlers, but it fell into obscurity and became overgrown until it was surveyed on a late-eighteenth-century estate map. In 1992, the site was bought by the Pembrokeshire Coast National Park, which has since supported an extensive education programme and long-term experimental archaeology project.

In 2001, a group of seventeen volunteers (including three chil-dren) agreed to participate in a reality TV show, *Surviving the Iron Age*, in which cameras followed their attempts to live together at Castell Henllys for seven weeks. While the BBC dubbed the series 'an experiment in living history', one of the participants described the experience as 'hell on earth'. Unfortunately, the filming took place during one of the wettest autumns since records began. The incessant rain made life very uncomfortable in the absence of a change of clothing and modern-day essentials such as toilet paper, deodorant and soap. Two of the children, aged 4 and 5, were withdrawn from the experiment by their mother after the young-est fell ill with food poisoning. Another participant withdrew after catching a bug.

Such experimental archaeology illustrates how surviving the Iron Age was no walk in the park. What became clear to the participants was that survival depended upon meeting the basic needs of shelter, food and water, but in ways that required a lot of collaboration, resilience and hard work. We take for granted turning a tap on to fill a kettle and fetching water from a nearby stream proved too much for the time travellers, who were frustrated by leaking buckets. This happened even though the producers provided a modern-day water tap. The daily grind of menial tasks took its toll within the group and friction soon developed. The humble wellington boot became a prized possession which they could not give up: it was a symbol of how far the twenty-first century had intervened in this living history project.

Water supply was a key factor in the location of hillforts. It is estimated that on the basis of the average person needing 2 litres of water a day to keep going, a hillfort of 100 people would require 44 gallons simply for drinking, let alone cooking. If animals were accommodated on site, then the water demands could be much higher. For these reasons, most hillforts were located near rivers or streams, although water may also have been obtained by catching rainwater, or from springs or wells.

Clegyr Boia hillfort (near St Davids), has two wells nearby: Ffynnon Dunawd and Ffynnon Llygaid. According to myth, the former is allegedly named after a young girl, Dunawd, who had her throat slit by her stepmother. The fountain sprang from where the blood was spilled. Ffynnon Llygaid, on the south side of Clegyr Boia, was reputed to clear eye problems.

For the Celts, the central hearth or fireplace was the basis for cooking food, boiling water, heating the roundhouse and the focal point around which they talked – interestingly, the Latin word *'focus'* means fireplace. The Welsh word *'aelwyd'* goes beyond hearth to convey the notion of family, or kinship, and home. The roundhouse image of cooking pots hanging from ceiling timbers over a central fire, with the family sharing stories, reinforces the social element of the hearth. The fire gave warmth while the rising smoke seeped through the thatched roof (rather than a distinct hole), keeping it dry and free from insects. The Roman historian Diodorus Siculus noted that the custom of the Celts was to sleep on wild animal skins on the ground 'and to wallow among bedfellows on either side'. Findings from Danesbury and other camps in the south of England suggest that larger roundhouses may also have accommodated various animals, including dogs and cats as pets or for pest control.

Radiocarbon dating shows that some of the Pembrokeshire hillforts are a few hundred years older than was once thought, and actually predate the Iron Age. Archaeologists have worked painstakingly in their reconstruction of the Castell Henllys round-houses, but it is important to remember that these are modern representations. For example, the walls were painted with lime wash for the purpose of improving visibility for modern visitors, but there is no evidence that this was done in the Iron Age. And even if it were so, the evidence would not have survived because of the acidic soil. The remains of many Iron Age homes are buried under trees and scrubland. The conventional end of the Iron Age is dated at the arrival of the Romans in the first century of the Christian era, although the transition to Roman rule was not a sudden, overnight affair.

ROMAN PEMBROKESHIRE,
AD 48–410

The Roman invasion of what we now call Wales began in earnest in AD 48, five years after they began their conquest of Britain. However, it took at least thirty years before the Romans had a semblance of control in the country through its camps and fortified settlements, notably Carmarthen in the west, Caerleon and Caerwent to control the south, and Chester in the north.

The Romans brought new thinking to these shores. The historian Robert Winder, in his book *Bloody Foreigners*, likens the Romans to 'modern-day expats, in warm, handsome haciendas, surrounded by walls to keep out the plebs'. For the Romans, civilised life meant centrally heated villas, amphitheatres, baths, exotic foods, wine and clothes. The extent to which the Celts were Romanised, or adopted Roman ways, by force or choice has long been debated. While Latin became the language of commerce in towns, this did not displace Brythonic, the Celtic language. In matters of worship, while the Romans brought different religious practices to Britain, including Christianity, the Celts continued to revere sacred wells, springs and lakes.

The Celts and Romans were not at constant loggerheads. Wars and tensions were interspersed with periods of relative peace. Carmarthen acted as the economic hub for West Wales, where trade was conducted between the Romans and the native population. As the archaeologist Barry Cunliffe argues, their relationship was as much about trade, cooperation and cultural exchange as violence and subjugation. For example, the Celts imported huge volumes of wine from the Romans in exchange for slaves. Another academic – on the eve of a Wales versus Italy rugby international – mischievously suggested that these nations had, in the long view of history, much more in common than people think.

Evidence for a Roman presence in Pembrokeshire has steadily accumulated over the centuries. In 1811, the antiquarian Richard Fenton mentioned the site of a Roman villa at Ford (Wolfscastle), where he found the remains of a bath, roofing tiles, iron nails and bricks. Further investigations found a Roman oil lamp, which is now in the Carmarthenshire Museum at Abergwili. Fragments of Roman brickwork and pottery have also been found at Castle Flemish (Ambleston). In the 1950s, another Roman villa was located at Trelissey (near Amroth), with the finds, including the head of a javelin, removed to Tenby Museum.

In the 1990s, during the construction of the Whitland bypass, aerial photographs and digital mapping identified the remains of a Roman road built in the AD 70s, heading west from Carmarthen towards Wiston, a civilian settlement (*vicus*) established around a Roman fort. The road stretches for around 17km just north of Haverfordwest and connects to the river-borne supply route of the Cleddau. Given that forts were typically located a day's march apart (20km or 15 miles), the first fort west of Carmarthen was likely to been sited around Whitland and the next one at Wiston.

For a large part, the present-day A40 follows the general course of the old Roman road. The Roman surveyors took advantage of a natural corridor from Carmarthen to Bancyfelin, then on to St Clears. From there, the road crosses hilly ground and bridges the eastern Cleddau at Llawhaden. Where possible, the Roman engineers avoided extensive woodlands to ensure a clear line of sight in case of ambush.

Evidence of quarry pits have been discovered along the route at Cotland Farm, north of Llawhaden. This stone formed the base of the road.

Other chance findings scattered through the county suggest that subsidiary roads extended from Haverfordwest to Fishguard and St Davids to make the most of trade by sea routes, which would be in keeping with the character of the Roman administrators.

Similarly, in the south of the county, a seaborne route probably connected Laugharne to Pendine, Amroth and Tenby, across to Caldey and then to Manorbier and Stackpole, round to Bosherston and Freshwater East, into the Haven to Angle, on up the River Cleddau to Pembroke and finally reaching Carew.

Roman finds from Whitesands Beach suggest that seaborne trading occurred. Findings elsewhere in Wales illustrate that luxury goods were imported from Europe, such as dates, wine, olives and olive oil, while wool and metals, such as lead and gold, were exported from Wales. We know the Romans mined gold at Dolaucothi in Carmarthenshire but there has also been speculation that gold was imported from Ireland following the recent discovery of a possible Roman route across the Preseli Hills heading towards the port of St Davids.

This idea is not a new one. Edward Lhuyd (or Lhwyd), the famous seventeenth-century antiquarian, visited Wales and reached the same conclusion, noting that Roman coins were often located in the Preseli area. Third-century Preseli slate has also been found at Caerleon, deposited on the surface of its quayside, but it is not clear whether this was used as ballast in boats or for roofing.

The Roman navy tends to be overlooked when we think of the Romans and their armies. It is likely that Agricola, the first-century Governor of Britain, deployed a detachment of his fleet based south of Bristol to keep an eye on the Welsh coast.

The Romans attempted conquest and settlement of Wales was a complex business. Wales at the time was not unified politically, comprising different tribes who shared similar cultures but did not respond in the same way to the Romans; whereas some fought bitterly, others engaged in diplomacy.

The Celts did not record their thoughts in writing, which means our view of them is skewed by what the Romans had to say. Archaeological evidence helps provide a more rounded picture but there are major gaps in what we know. Over a span of 360 or so years, retracing the infrastructure of forts and roads, let alone social relationships, remains challenging. It is a fair assumption that the further people lived from the main Roman settlements, such as Carmarthen, the more life went on much as before the Romans arrived. This was particularly likely for isolated communities in remote Pembrokeshire. We do know that the pressures on the Roman Empire exerted in mainland Europe meant that troops were withdrawn from Britain beginning in the late fourth century AD.

EARLY MEDIEVAL PEMBROKESHIRE, AD 410–854

The centuries that followed the end of Roman rule in Britain witnessed the emergence of Wales as a nation. Wales had its own rulers and respected laws, administrative boundaries started to take shape, and St Davids Cathedral led the Celtic Church. Christian teaching influenced what people wore, ate and drank, how they spoke, travelled and entertained themselves. In the case of eating, for example, Fridays, Saturdays and many Wednesdays were 'fish days'. This meant that people could only eat fish, based on the belief that warm-blooded animal meat should be avoided as a sign of respect for the sacrifice of Jesus, who is said to have died on a Friday. There were also 'fast days' to be observed and during Advent (the forty days leading up to Christmas) no meat could be eaten. Holy days, religious festivals and observances dominated the calendar.

AGE OF THE SAINTS

The fifth and sixth centuries were a time of considerable missionary activity. In AD 597, the arrival of Augustine at Canterbury traditionally marks the beginnings of the Catholic Church under the Pope's universal direction. Christianity was already present in Pembrokeshire, brought by missionaries from Ireland and the Continent.

Historian Gwyn Davies points out that while some of the saints were attracted to the self-disciplined, isolated monastic life afforded at such locations as Caldey Island, others pursued evangelical and pastoral aspects of their faith as part of their '*clas*', or community.

Christianity left its mark in Pembrokeshire through standing crosses, churches, abbeys and priories (Figure 6). Gaelic missionaries buried their dead and marked the graves with a monolith, on which they inscribed the name of the deceased in an Irish script known as Ogham. This is named after the legendary Irish god, Ogma.

Among the surviving stones are those at Cilgerran, St Dogmaels, Steynton and Caldey Island. The Cilgerran example in St Llawddog's Church bears the inscription, 'Of Trenegussus, son of Macutrenus, lies here'. Many of these stones are marked with a cross, indicating their association with Christianity.

The Monastic Wales Project, led by Professor Janet Burton, has identified fifty-nine monastic sites in Wales which operated between the eleventh and sixteenth centuries, including six in Pembrokeshire: Caldey Priory, the Benedictine Priory in Pembroke, the Pill Priory (near Milford Haven), the Knights Hospitaller in Slebech, the Augustinian Priory of Haverfordwest and St Dogmaels Abbey. But there were other monastic and religious houses in the earlier period. On the island of Gateholm, for example, archaeologists found evidence of rectangular huts arranged around a courtyard which they think are the remains of a sixth-century monastic settlement.

Christian heritage is noted in the placename prefixes '*Llan*', which, in the early days, referred to the land around the church, and '*Capel*' (for example, Capel Brynach and Capel Degwel). The saints or holy men after which many churches are named each built up a cache of stories. These particularly mattered in an age when storytelling took priority over the written word in people's lives.

St Brynach was an Irish saint who lived most of his life in West Wales and spoke to angels on Carn Ingli, cloaked in heather and gorse, where he would spend hours in prayer and contemplation. This became known as the Mount of Angels. Apparently, he could also talk to animals, once convincing a team of deer to bring tree trunks from the forest to build his monastery. Several churches are named after him, the most famous located in Nevern. The ruins of another can be seen at Cwm-yr-Eglwys near Dinas Cross.

St Caradoc, from Breconshire, had a reputation for sanctity. After his body had been interred at St Davids Cathedral, several years later, the historian William of Malmesbury tried to cut off a finger to keep as a holy relic. Understandably, Caradoc's hand jerked away.

St Govan was probably a sixth-century Irish hermit, a contemporary of St David, who lived in a cave near Bosherston (now St Govan's Head). His choice of home was said to have followed his escape from an attack by Irish pirates, when the cliff opened up and left a fissure big enough for him to hide until they left. The cell, or 'penitential bed', was said to be so tight that Govan left an impression of his ribs on the rock as he lay down. This cell is within the rocks close to the thirteenth or fourteenth-century chapel (restored in the 1980s). One legend suggests that St Govan was Sir Gawain, Arthur's Knight of the Round Table.

Fig. 6 Haverfordwest Priory. (*Fenton, 1811, p. 206*)

St Justinian, who was a sixth-century hermit living on Ramsey Island, was murdered by disgruntled monks or servants. According to one story, they beheaded him, only to find that he picked his head up, placed it under his arm and walked across to the mainland. He was then buried a site later named after him, St Justinian's, opposite his island home.

St Sampson was the son of a noble family from South Wales, born in the early AD 500s. His might was such that he reputedly used his little finger to place the capstone on top of the cromlech, Carreg Sampson, or Sampson's Stone, near Abercastle. The finger is supposed to be buried on Ynys y Castell, the rocky island opposite, guarding the entrance to the bay.

The mental picture of medieval monasteries is typically one of monks engaged in silent contemplation, prayer, conscientiously copying manuscripts with quill in hand or keeping bees. St David is said to have allowed St Damnoc, a keen beekeeper, to return to his homeland of Ireland because he was homesick. Legend suggests that a swarm of bees followed him and were the first to arrive in the Emerald Isle.

Reputedly, those wishing to join St David were received naked, as if in a shipwreck, and kept waiting for some time before admission. Their diet consisted of bread, herbs and water. Meat was avoided because it fuelled lustful tendencies.

There were other temptations, however. One legend has it that a pagan chief's wife told her maids to go and stand naked in front of the monks, play games and use lewd words to tempt them from their vows. St David and his monks worked with their heads bowed to avoid eye contact. The same legend says that the pagans' camp was later destroyed by fire.

The monastic communities played a key part in wider society. The great medieval churchman and scholar, Gerald of Wales, describes how monks kept sheep and bred horses, ran farms and mills, reclaimed land and felled trees. They cared for the poor and the sick and provided hospitality to strangers. They maintained roads and travelled to mainland Europe to sell wool and negotiate deals. The writer Michael Pye makes the point in *The Edge of the World* that holiness was not the first thing anyone noticed when visiting monasteries, which typically resembled small towns, forts and strongrooms and were fair game for any raider.

Fig. 7 St Govan's Chapel. (*Roscoe, 1811, frontispiece*)

Monasteries were important seats of learning and the preservation of heritage. In monastic schools, subjects such as grammar, astronomy, music, logic and arithmetic were studied. Outside the monasteries and royal courts, however, literacy was not a skill that concerned most people in an age when perhaps less than one in ten men and fewer women could read.

Asser was Pembrokeshire's most famous medieval scholar-monk. In about AD 885, he took up King Alfred of Wessex's invite to join his court as a royal adviser on condition he could also spend time at St Davids. In return for Asser's wisdom, the king agreed to be 'in all ways helpful to St Davids, as far as his power extended'. Asser wrote a flattering biography of Arthur which did much to shape the Victorian view of him as 'the most perfect character in history'.

HOLY WELLS

There are around 700 holy wells in Wales, approximately a third of which are in Pembrokeshire. Among the most famous is St Govan's, near the chapel which bears his name. In fact, there are two wells: one inside the small chapel and one outside, towards the shoreline. Modern-day visitors can descend the fifty-two stone steps (said to be uncountable) to the chapel and wells, although the exterior well is now covered by a small stone house and lintel.

Visitors have long been attracted to the site. In 1662, the tourist John Ray referred to the well as 'being famous for the Cure of all Diseases'. In 1775, Sir Thomas Cullum visited the well and spoke to a poor woman and her husband, who had walked 40 miles from Carmarthen seeking a cure for his bad hip. Cullum commented on the custom of leaving money to the priestess of the chapel, but she was absent on his visit. He parted with a cynical swipe, 'It may not be very difficult for this well to support its reputation, if visited by People who can walk near 40 miles and back again!' Richard Fenton, visiting in the 1800s, referred to crippled visitors leaving their crutches as votive offerings on the altar.

Many of the holy wells are associated with miraculous tales. St David created wells by banging his staff on the soil or shedding tears. Rituals were performed at the sites of wells, such as dropping in bent pins, which was regarded as a cure for sore eyes and other ailments. The waters from Letterston's Well near Fishguard were sold for a shilling a bottle.

Wells, of course, provided an essential source of pure water over the centuries before the advent of piped supplies and reservoirs.

Lizzie Roberts recalled the 'lovely water' she collected from her village well in Rosemarket as a child in the 1880s. She also remembered people going to bathe their eyes in the neighbouring Leonard's Well because it was well known for its healing qualities.

MEDIEVAL WELSH LAWS

We get a sense of what medieval life was like by considering the surviving Welsh Laws. Tradition has it that Hywel Dda, or Hywel the Good, born around AD 880, codified these in the tenth century at the White House (now Whitland), where around 1,000 dignitaries gathered from all parts of the country.

Hywel Dda was the much-respected King of Deheubarth, which covered south-west Wales. A Latin translation of the laws was later presented for the papal blessing in Rome. The earliest surviving manuscripts of the laws date to the thirteenth century and were used by lawyers of the day.

The significance of these laws is that they were not manifestations of a powerful elite or designed to protect the state. Rather, they were social laws built on fostering good relationships among the people and to protect them. In practice, the legal system differed to the one that operated in England. For example, if someone stole £100 from another person in England, this was a criminal act prosecuted by the Crown and, if found guilty, the offender was likely to be sentenced to six months' imprisonment. Generally, the victim did not receive £100 in return, although there were some exceptions, like restitution, which had to be ordered. In Welsh Law, the default position was that the money had to be repaid by some means or another. Moreover, the Welsh Laws operated according to natural reason. The process was for the two opposing parties to try and settle their differences. If they could not, then compromise should be sought. Only after these two steps had been taken could parties pursue the matter through the court.

The Welsh Laws have been widely praised for their reasonableness and civility in avoiding the barbaric practices known in England, such as trial by ordeal or trial by combat. The former required an accused person to plunge his arm into boiling water, walk barefooted over red-hot irons or carry molten metal in his hand. If the wounds festered after seven days, he was found guilty, whereas if they healed, he was declared innocent. The Welsh Laws also avoided the use of the stocks, where the guilty were placed in the public square and subjected to ridicule. Trial by combat was used throughout Europe to settle disputes in the absence of witnesses or a confession. It involved individuals engaging in duels, with the winner proclaimed to be in the right.

Most famously, the Welsh Laws gave men and women equal rights of ownership. Marriages did not have to be sanctioned by the Church because they were considered civil agreements. Nothing was said about 'marriages being made in heaven'. Divorce was possible for both parties, although there were conditions. For example, if a woman left her husband without his consent, she would lose all her moveable possessions if this happened within the first seven years, but she could take everything with her after this time. A wife could leave her husband if he was impotent, a leper and even if he had bad breath.

Other egalitarian features of the laws were that bastards were given the same rights as legitimate siblings, marriage was to happen by common consent, land was to be divided equally between spouses on separation and among all children on the deaths of their parents. We know little about the extent to which such legislation was enacted, but the principles were certainly ahead of their time.

5

THE VIKINGS IN PEMBROKESHIRE

From around AD 790, the Pembrokeshire coast was used by sea raiders from Scandinavia, seeking shelter as they raided Ireland. They succeeded in making Dublin their stronghold from which to launch further raids. The first recorded attack on Wales did not occur until fifty years later, in north Wales. Around the same time, in AD 854, a chieftain called Ubba, or Hubba, wintered his twenty-three ships in the haven of Milford. Hubba gave his name to the local village, Hubberston.

The word 'Viking' comes from the old Norse language '*vík*', which means bay, from which seaborne raiders and adventurers set out to explore new worlds. The Vikings established Dublin as a strong base from which to launch westerly raids into south and West Wales. They had no qualms about ransacking religious houses, where they knew treasures were stored. Between 967 and 1091, the Vikings struck St Davids Cathedral eleven times and tradition has it that the cathedral lay desolate for seven years before the Christian community was re-established.

Very few Viking objects have been discovered in Pembrokeshire. One notable exception was in 1991, when a diver exploring a shipwreck off the Smalls Reef found a decorated brass Viking sword guard, which was dated to around 1100. The sword was probably for ceremonial use and belonged to a leader, given its elaborative design. The area around the site of the scattered wreck is now protected in law.

While the Vikings were known for their maritime skills, they were equally gifted horsemen, craftworkers, poets and traders. Their leaders were also politicians, caught up in the complex picture of local power struggles in the eighth, ninth and tenth centuries.

The Viking threat was not an isolated one – Deheubarth was also subject to attacks from rival kingdoms, notably Gwynedd and Glamorgan, as well as English lords targeting moveable wealth such as cattle. To illustrate the complexities, while Hywel ap Edwin, as ruler of Deheubarth, defeated the Vikings in 1043 in a battle near Carmarthen, he was overrun by forces from Gwynedd, who also seized his unnamed wife. The following year, Hywel returned from exile with a hired force of Irish Viking fighters in a failed attempt to regain his kingdom.

It was not uncommon for Viking mercenaries to join forces with rulers in South Wales to raid lands across the English border. On other occasions, the Vikings took captives for ransom and held them in Dublin.

We know very little about the Viking presence in Pembrokeshire, other than their use of shoreline villages as winter homes for their fleet. One suggestion is that Milford Haven comes from the Norse '*Melrfjordr*', a combination of '*melr*' (sandbank) and '*fjord*' (inlet). The islands of Skokholm, Grassholm, Caldey and Skomer, as well as rocks such as Goscar, Emsger and Tusker, are all Norse placenames. The association with coastal features (islands, bays, nooks, rocks, sandbanks) is not surprising, given the Vikings' seafaring skills.

Some settlements are linked to personal names (Haroldston – *Haraldr*; Wolfscastle – *Ulf*; Freystrop – *Freyr*). However, it is not clear whether these originated as pre-existing Welsh townships (*trefi*) which were given as rewards to invading Viking leaders. While Scandinavian names entered the English language, few have any correspondence with the Welsh names given to places, which suggests that there was limited contact between the different language groups of the time.

Despite their considerable skills and prowess, the Vikings did not take control of Pembrokeshire and were unable, or unwilling, to overcome the power of the Welsh kings. Still, the nineteenth-century historian Edward Laws suggested that the Vikings did leave a threefold legacy among the 'Little Englanders' of south Pembrokeshire: their horsemanship, sailing and habits of heavy drinking.

6

THE NORMANS
AND FLEMINGS

We know a lot more about the Viking descendants who gave their name to the region of north-west France (Normandy), where they settled in the tenth century, prior to their invasion of England and Wales. The Normans were responsible for transforming Pembrokeshire from a Welsh-speaking kingdom to an English-speaking shire. Norman/English placenames include Puncheston, Rudbaxton, Haroldston, Tavernspite and New Hedges. Pembroke, Tenby, Haverfordwest and Newport also owe their existence to the Normans.

In 1081, William the Conqueror (Figure 8) visited St Davids Cathedral. The contemporary *Welsh Chronicles* suggest that he came on pilgrimage, but this didn't prevent him from bringing an army, just to be on the safe side. Laws described 'a force the like of which had not been seen in Pembrokeshire since Roman days'. He compared it to a triumphant march, with William viewed as 'an instrument of God in that he crushed the accursed Saxon'. The likelihood is that the pilgrimage was a cover for French-speaking William to sound out Welsh-speaking Rhys ap Tewdwr, the new Prince of Deheubarth. Whatever tensions existed, in the presence of translators they managed to agree a deal to respect the borders between their kingdoms.

William honoured his agreement with Rhys. However, following the death of both leaders, this disintegrated in the subsequent reigns of William II (Rufus) and Henry I, and the Norman barons began to impose their authority in Wales.

Given that William married Matilda, Princess of Flanders, it was no surprise that a group of Flemings accompanied the Normans during their invasion and that some Flemish knights were rewarded with land and estates following the Norman Conquest. King Henry I arranged for around 2,500 Flemings to be sent to Pembrokeshire to 'quell the unruly Welsh' and establish a cloth trade. One contemporary recorded in 1134 that the Flemish 'butchered' the Welsh 'like dogs, without any regard for humanity, whenever they could track them out in the woods and caves in which they lurked'. Benjamin Malkin, writing in 1807, identified a mountainous tract over the Preseli Hills as the Fleming Way, so named because the Flemings could 'avoid the snares which the natives were continually laying for them in the narrow passes and plains'.

The Flemish settled in south Pembrokeshire, occupying Roch and Tancredston, in the west, the central villages of Wiston and Llawhaden, and the more northern Letterston and Little Newcastle. Wiston originated from the wonderfully named 'Wizo the Flem', who built the village's motte-and-bailey castle.

It has been customary to see the Flemish legacy in terms of the round-chimneyed houses in south Pembrokeshire, with suggested examples at Flimston, Monkton and St Florence (Figure 9). As early as 1902, however, this was challenged by Thomas Dawes, local historian and headmaster of Pembroke Dock County School. In his book *The Flemings in Pembrokeshire*, Dawes

Fig.8 Portrait of William the Conqueror from the Bayeux Tapestry. (*Laws, 1888, p.95*)

Fig. 9 Round chimneys, wrongly attributed to the Flemings. (*Laws, 1888, pp. 116 & 119*)

argued, 'There is not a scrap of evidence to connect them with the Flemings [...] Flemish chimneys do not exist in Flanders.'

Laws suggested that the greatest Flemish legacy lay in the physique of the people of south Pembrokeshire, 'fair haired, light eyed women [...] if young, a complexion of strawberries and cream'. In 2015, a DNA test revealed a high probability that Peter Cousins, a local Pembrokeshire man, indeed had Flemish forefathers.

While the Flemings may have been ruthless colonists, they were eventually outnumbered by English settlers, mostly from the West Country. English slowly became the dominant language in south Pembrokeshire. Over the centuries, a distinctive dialect has emerged based on a mix of English, Flemish, Irish and Scandinavian. Words include 'tamping' (angry), 'kift' (awkward), 'culm' (a small piece of coal), 'catchypole' (tadpole) and 'sea parrot' (puffin).

The Pembrokeshire Welsh dialect, spoken mainly in the northern part of the county, also has unique vocabulary; for example, '*feidir*' rather than '*lôn*', which is used in other parts of south-west Wales for lane, '*rhocyn*' for lad and '*claw*' for hedge. In English, the British Library holds a fascinating audio recording from 1976 of an old Pembrokeshire couple talking about traditional haymaking. As they speak, they pronounce the 'r' sound after a vowel, for example, never, horse, barn, hayguard, corn and so on.[2] These are what linguists call 'rhotic speakers'.

Dialect remains a point of interest. In 2021, when the true crime drama *The Pembrokeshire Murders* was aired on television, viewers took to social media to discuss the accuracy of the dialect, pointing out that words such as 'Mam' are typically heard above rather than below the *Landsker*.

PEMBROKESHIRE'S CASTLES

The most obvious Norman legacy is their castles. Sources vary on the exact number of castles in Pembrokeshire. Writing in 1603,

2   https://www.bl.uk/collection-items/dyfed-dialect-mr-and-mrs-m-traditional-haymaking-practice

the Pembrokeshire antiquary George Owen noted nineteen, the authoritative *Pembrokeshire County History* mentions fifty-five (including six which have vanished), the respected historian J. Geraint Jenkins refers to sixteen major castles and sixty minor ones, while the Wikipedia entry identifies eighteen. These differences are largely due to how castles are defined and distinguished from other buildings, such as fortified manor houses or stately homes. The important point is that the Normans valued the land sufficiently to build castles in such numbers.

Nowadays, castles conjure up images of bows and arrows, turrets, knights in shining armour, damsels, boiling oil, sieges, catapults and battering rams. In reality, typical castle life was far less dramatic with prolonged periods of peace and humdrum activity. Castles were local administrative centres where taxes were collected and courts held, while also serving as homes for the wealthy and mini-communities with gardens, stables, bakeries and granaries. Pembroke even had its own subterranean cave (Wogan's Cavern) and mill pond.

Castles then were not simply places of refuge in hard times but where people lived, entertained, showed off the latest fashions, drank, slept and conceived children. In the case of Pembroke, the Tudor dynasty began with the birth there of Henry Tudor.

Pembrokeshire certainly has a wide range of castles. The earliest earth-and-timber castles were built by the Normans around 1100, either as motte-and-bailey or ringwork varieties. These were quick and cheap to build but had a limited lifespan and were replaced by or evolved into more substantial stone structures, as was the case at Llawhaden.

The first castle the Normans built in the county was probably at Pembroke in 1093, an enclosure-style castle with a great keep (Figure 10). Then there were other major castles which were owned by Norman lords loyal to the Crown, such as Cilgerran, built by Roger, Earl of Montgomery.

Most of the Anglo-Normans castles were built along the coast or within inlets, so that they could be supplied quickly by sea. North of the Preseli Hills, the Welsh built numerous earthwork castles themselves, such as Castell Pen-yr-allt (at Cilgerran), Eglwyswrw and Castell Dyffryn Mawr (near Crymych), which has some stonework remains.

Fig. 10 Pembroke Castle. (*Roscoe, 1837, plate XXX*)

While some castles have long disappeared, others were strength-ened and later transformed into fortified manors, becoming domestic homes over subsequent centuries. Picton Castle, 5 miles south-east of Haverfordwest, is important because it illustrates the change from a medieval fortress to a Victorian stately home (Figure 11).

The Normans built a motte-and-bailey castle here to overlook the River Cleddau. In 1302, Sir John Wogan built the present fortified home. He held a prominent position in Ireland and was inspired by Irish hall-keep architecture to raise a rectangular keep containing a great hall and undercroft, with four corner towers. In 1469, Picton Castle passed to the Philipps family, although little work was carried out until 1697 when a balustraded causeway was added. Further changes transformed what was described as a dark fortress into a Regency mansion with the addition of new accommodation, a drawing room, warm furnishings, portraits and a library, with its curved bookcases, secret panels and high-quality workmanship.

The beautiful grounds are largely the work of the designer Thomas Rowlands who, in the early nineteenth century, built lodges, iron railings, an impressive courtyard, a stable block and a model farm. Wogan's original hall-keep and undercroft remain as a reminder of this transformation. For Richard Fenton, who visited in the 1800s, what made Picton Castle special was the fact that it had always been inhabited since Norman times, 'not by owls and bats, but by lords of its own, men eminent in their day as warriors, as statesmen, and as Christians'.

Carew Castle is one of the most attractive in Wales, situated along the River Carew and overlooking the crossing point. The castle was founded around 1100 by Gerald de Windsor, Constable of nearby Pembroke Castle. The Old Tower remains from this period.

Manorbier Castle is most famously associated with the priest and writer, Gerald of Wales, grandson of Gerald de Windsor. Given that this was his birthplace, Gerald naturally considered it was the best spot in Wales, with the air like 'heaven's breath'.

In 1188, Gerald accompanied Archbishop Baldwin of Canterbury on a recruitment tour for the Third Crusade to recapture Jerusalem. Strangely, while they preached in Latin and French and most ordinary people could understand neither language, the audience responses were reportedly far more positive than when a translator was present. The first to 'take the cross' in Wales was Gerald himself, no doubt in a prearranged publicity move, when he seized a cloth cross after Baldwin had finished his sermon at New Radnor, during the start of the tour of Wales.

Fig. 11 Picton Castle. (*Fenton, 1811, opposite p.277*)

Gerald had most success at Haverfordwest. At the time, the town had a cosmopolitan feel, with the presence of Flemings, Welsh, Irish and Anglo-Normans. As a centre for the wool trade, merchants had close connections to Europe and were therefore receptive to the message about fighting for the shared Christian faith and heritage. The Flemings had previously fought in the Second Crusade and had a reputation for bravery. Moreover, fighting a common enemy offered the prospect of setting aside differences between the Welsh and Flemings.

And then there was the persuasive appeal of miracles. Gerald referred to the first of these at Haverfordwest. The son of a blind old woman took a piece of turf, where the archbishop was standing, home to his mother. When she pressed it against her face, her sight was restored.

Such miraculous tales trigger cynicism in our largely secular world. In the Middle Ages, however, people's view of the world was shaped by the Church, superstition and magic. They welcomed any potential relief in life, particularly given its precarious nature. Disease and plague were constant threats, which some attributed to God's punishment for people's sins and waywardness.

PLAGUE

Most devastating of the plagues was 'the deadly pestilence', which swept through Europe between 1347 and 1350. It is nearly impossible for us to imagine the fear and pain that people experienced when they witnessed their loved ones dying in agony in a matter of days, if not hours. The outbreak of the Covid-19 pandemic illustrated the wide-ranging impact a sudden virus can have on society, including the economy, transport, employment, recreation, education and health. However, this pales into insignificance compared to the Black Death, which claimed at least one in four lives in Wales, even though those living in the scattered, remote farmhouses in northern parts of Pembrokeshire probably had better survival chances compared to the more populated south.

What amounted to the largest infectious disease catastrophe in human history has conventionally been attributed to fleas hosted by the black rat. However, forensic archaeologists now think that the bacteria may originally have been spread by marmots or squirrels in central Asia. The pneumonic form was caught by breathing in the infection.

People had to live with the uncertainty of the plague returning unannounced. In 1348, sailors were said to have brought the plague to Haverfordwest on a market day from an infected ship in Milford Haven. Among the first victims were the Haverfordwest customs officials and members of the major landowning families, such as John Perrot of Popton, Walter Scurlage of Bangeston (near Pembroke) and Nicholas Shirburn of Angle.

St Davids Cathedral appealed for new priests to fill the gaps caused by those who fell victim to the plague. Recruitment was difficult because of the inherent dangers posed when priests were in such close contact with the afflicted in administering the last rites. The death of a priest was a big blow to the community. Pembroke lost two of its priests between March and June 1349, although the shortage presented unexpected promotional opportunities. The priest in the parish of Steynton had only been in post for three months before being appointed vicar. Sadly, in some cases, those who survived the Black Death fell victims to a second pestilence of 1361–62. This included John Shirburn, from a family dubbed 'ancient lords of Angle', who died at the age of 31, leaving his 10-year-old daughter, Alice, to succeed him.

If he had time and the health to do so, the town crier or bellman tolled for plague victims. He also announced other news, including victories or celebrations. The famous street cries of 'Oyez, oyez, oyez!' derived from the Anglo-Norman command, 'Listen!' In pre-modern times, bells were an important means of communication. According to legend, St David carried his own personal bell called *Bangu* as he travelled around the country, calling people to worship. The present bell frame in the tower of St Davids Cathedral used timber felled in the 1380s and is the oldest in Wales. Haverfordwest became a town of bells, given its three parish churches along with the belltowers in the friary and the priory. Even with the advent of nineteenth-century mass communication, such as newspapers, the town crier continued to play a role in spreading the news. Among the highlights of the nineteenth-century Tenby bellman was the capture of a 20ft man-eating shark.

7

TUDOR PEMBROKESHIRE, 1485–1603

One of the most delightful fictional films set in Pembrokeshire is *Bus to Bosworth* (1976), directed by John Hefin. It tells the story of a village school retracing the route Henry Tudor and his army took in 1485 on their way to Bosworth Field in Leicestershire. The opening scene sees the schoolmaster (Kenneth Griffith) emerge from the sea in the role of Henry Tudor and kneel on the beach at Mill Bay to offer a prayer in Latin, Welsh and English, proclaiming his rightful inheritance to the royal crown of England from Richard III. His nationalistic assistant Miss Evans (Rachel Thomas) calls for his followers (the schoolchildren) to give three cheers for Henry Tudor and three boos for 'wicked' Richard III, forcing Griffith to have a quiet word with her, 'I really think the latter is unnecessary and let us hold to the historical facts'.

HENRY TUDOR

What are the historical facts? On 7 August 1485, the 28-year-old Henry Tudor landed at the mouth of the Milford Haven water-way, having spent most of his life exiled in France. Henry Tudor's choice of Mill Bay was no accident. Born in Pembroke Castle, he was familiar with the land where his uncle, Jasper Tudor, retained local contacts. During the Wars of the Roses (1455–87) Jasper was stripped of his lands by the Yorkist King Edward IV but continued to shelter young Henry, who represented the Lancastrians' best hope of reclaiming the throne.

In 1471, Jasper and his nephew were the most wanted people in the country when they were smuggled into Tenby from a besieged Pembroke Castle. They were hidden by the White family until a ship was ready for them. Underground passages, which still survive, probably helped Henry and Jasper to reach the harbour undetected. On 2 June, under the cover of darkness, they set sail for France but were forced by the weather to land in Brittany, which was then a separate nation.

The historian John Davies points out that Henry's return to Wales was not treated with any great enthusiasm nor rush to join his army marching to Bosworth. But neither was it opposed. Henry Tudor was supported by the major landowner Sir Rhys ap Thomas, who in return was promised the governance of Wales if Henry claimed the crown.

During the Wars of the Roses, Sir Rhys ap Thomas originally vowed to support King Richard III against the exiled Henry Tudor, declaring that the latter would only land back in Wales 'over my belly'. In 1485, when Henry Tudor returned, the story goes that Sir Rhys eased his conscience by hiding under Mullock Bridge as Henry and his entourage rode over. Sir Rhys ap Thomas then took his huge army to fight on Henry's side at Bosworth Field.

The victorious Henry duly rewarded Rhys with a knighthood and, in celebration, a great tournament was held at the castle in 1507. It was spread over five days and attended by 600 nobles, including the leading Pembrokeshire families headed by Sir Thomas Perrot and Sir John Wogan.

The traditional interpretation of why Henry was victorious at Bosworth

Fig. 12 Eighteenth-century print of Henry VII. (*Hume, 1754*)

highlights the decisive role of the Stanley brothers: William switched sides and deployed his army against Richard, while his elder brother Thomas adopted a 'wait and see' attitude before backing Henry as the most likely winner. It may also have been the case, however, that the Stanley brothers were even more calculating and sought to settle a long-running feud over land with James Harrington, who was one Richard's closest supporters.

For the Pembrokeshire gentry, Henry Tudor's victory and crowning as king was regarded as a great success story (Figure 12). At least, this was the view of George Owen, who saw Henry as 'a Pembrokeshire man'. Owen was writing at the end of the Tudor dynasty and he could look back to the rise of the Welsh gentry and their increasing career opportunities in London.

Henry VII revived the Welsh dragon on his coat of arms, an important symbolic gesture. In 1496, John Morgan was appointed as Bishop of St Davids, the first Welshman for more than a century. But Henry VII did little to combat the lawlessness and misrule that was reported to prevail in Wales. Moreover, his Welshness has been over-exaggerated: as John Davies points out, by descent, he was a quarter Welsh, a quarter French and half English, and it was his English blood that legitimised his claim to the throne.

The modern-day views of the Welsh people towards Henry Tudor are ambivalent. In 2002, the general public voted him only fifty-third in a poll to find Wales's greatest heroes, attracting a mere 142 votes. In 2018, a four-year campaign to erect a statue of Henry Tudor outside Pembroke Castle proved successful, although this is, of course, where he was born and is located in an overwhelmingly English-speaking part of the county. Efforts to commemorate him may not have been so successful in the north of Pembrokeshire, Ceredigion or Gwynedd.

Nonetheless, as king, Henry was generally well respected for establishing a peaceful reign. He was a shrewd operator in both his statecraft and personal life. When his ambassadors visited Joanna of Aragon to ascertain her potential as a prospective wife, they were instructed to ask twenty-four intimate questions, including whether hair grew on her top lip and the strength of her bodily smell. Just to be certain, they were also to solicit a portrait 'done very secretly' and shipped back to England as quickly as possible. Such antics were not uncommon in an age when portraits played a key part in courtship. They are perhaps more readily associated with Henry VII's second son, who was to prove a far more divisive ruler than his father.

HENRY VIII AND THE REFORMATION

George Owen suggested that Henry VIII had been instructed by his father to have 'a special care' for the Welsh. By and large, this did not happen. On the contrary, under Henry VIII's reign, legislation was passed in 1536 which meant that the Welsh language was banned from the law courts and Welsh speakers barred from public office, although by 1542 the Welsh were at least represented in Parliament. While the so-called Acts of Union have been heavily criticised for their restrictions on the Welsh language, they opened up opportunities for the Welsh gentry to advance their power and interests, whether as Justices of the Peace, Members of Parliament or through pursuing new trade openings.

Henry VIII's reign ushered in a period of increasing religious tensions following the annulment of his marriage to Catherine of Aragon in 1533, and the Act of Supremacy the following year, which made the king the head of the Church in England. The writer Rudyard Kipling described Henry VIII as 'naturally a cruel man, drunk with pride and power'. In his *History of England*, published in 1911, the motive for dissolving the monasteries was greed, irrespective of claims about immorality and corruption among the monks (Figure 13). Most of the

Fig. 13 The Dissolution of the Monasteries, depicted in 1911. *(Fletcher and Kipling, 1911, p.119)*

gentry and merchant classes had no qualms over the attacks on the Catholic Church, as they were envious of its power, which was wielded, for example, through financial dues and Church courts. There was also the small matter of the consequences of publicly speaking out of turn and facing the king's wrath.

Local politics also came into play. In Haverfordwest, although the Dominicans and Augustinians were both religious orders within Roman Catholicism, their relations were strained. William Barlow was the radical prior of the Augustinians, appointed in 1534 by Anne Boleyn, second wife of Henry VIII and Marquess of Pembroke, which made her a significant landowner in Wales. Barlow preached against papal authority in English affairs, echoing Thomas Cromwell's position as adviser to Henry VIII. He also attacked the Augustinians for venerating an image of the Virgin Mary. They retaliated, alleging that Barlow's sins included illicit relations with an abbess of a Norfolk nunnery.

Despite such bickering, there was little appetite in Pembrokeshire for opposing Henry's reforms, unlike the north of England where the old Catholic faith remained strong. By the time Henry VIII's officials closed the Augustinian priory in Haverfordwest, it housed only four canons and the prior. Barlow had already moved on, holding various offices before his appointment in 1536 as Bishop of St Davids. He soon removed relics and the shrine of St David and arranged for old books to be torn up to make way for new Protestant prayer books. The fact that the cathedral holds the tomb of Henry VIII's grandfather, Edmund Tudor, may have mitigated the extent of the destruction.

Excavations 450 years later gave clues as to how Haverfordwest Priory was demolished. Piles of glass and lead from the priory windows were unearthed and showed signs of being melted down to form ingots, one of which survived bearing the crown's stamp and number; in other words, these were part of the monarch's property, ready to be transported for sale. Another hint of the destruction is the circular indent on the tiled floor, perhaps struck by the fallen bell. Robbers took slabs from the nave floor, garden and cloister to be sold or reused in other buildings. Sir John Perrot, the local magnate, may have seized these to repair his nearby house at Haroldston. Sections of the walls also appear to have been systematically dismantled.

The burning of W.Nicole at Hereford-weft in Wales.

Fig. 14 The burning of William Nichol. (*Foxe, 1576*)

The most obvious impact of the Reformation on people's lives was that certain practices came to an end. There were no more candles lit at Candlemas, while altars, images, incense, holy water and vestments disappeared in churches. English replaced Latin as the language of service, although for Welsh-speaking parishioners in north Pembrokeshire such a change is unlikely to have made the sermons any more intelligible. For Pembrokeshire clergymen, one change did matter – they could now legally take a wife.

In 1553, Mary became queen, following the execution of Lady Jane Grey, who lasted barely nine days. Mary sought to reverse the English Reformation and forcefully restore Catholicism.

One of three Protestant martyrs in Wales was William Nichol who, in 1558, was burned at the stake in Haverfordwest (Figure 14). Little is known about his beliefs or life, although in Foxe's *Book of Martyrs*, he is described as 'so simple and good that many esteemed him half foolish'. The burning was marked in the town by a red granite pillar, erected in 1912, with the inscription: 'The noble army of Martyrs praise thee. On this spot William Nichol of this town was burnt at the stake for the truth, April 9th 1558.' In November of that year, Mary died from influenza and was succeeded by Elizabeth I.

Tudor Pembrokeshire had its fair share of committed Protestants and papists, although the extent to which ordinary people practised what was preached is difficult to know. On the one hand, the Tudor Age remained a highly religious one, yet people were also very superstitious, especially about health and fertility.

'Wise men' or wizards (*Dyn Hysbys*) were said to possess the powers of breaking spells and undoing evil, as well as revealing the unknown. They used charms to heal and protect; for example, placing written messages in Latin and English in cork bottles hidden in buildings housing sick animals. Most communities knew of an old woman who, it was believed, had the power to cast spells over people or animals.

In his book on *Pembrokeshire Wizards and Witches*, Brian John suggests that they may have inherited some of the skills and occult knowledge of the druids, passed down through the ages. According to John, 'Every self-respecting town, village and hamlet had at least one witch.' Significantly, despite persecution, witches continued to play a role well into the nineteenth century, providing locals with herbal remedies, foretelling their futures and exorcising ghosts from their homes.

The Church and the lord of the manor had the power to punish witches. The earliest recorded case in Wales dates to 1502 when John Morgan, the Bishop of St Davids, imprisoned Tangwystl ferch Gwilym in the episcopal castle at Lawhadden. She was accused of living in 'open adultery' with Thomas Wyrriot. He managed to rescue her and duly left his wife, who died afterwards, it was rumoured from sorcery. Tangwystl was again imprisoned and then banished. Enraged by this, she contacted another witch named Margaret Hackett from Bristol to put a spell on the bishop. Before he died, Morgan instructed that a chapel be built over his grave in the cathedral. This did not happen, although visitors can see Morgan's carved stone tomb.

Churchgoers indulged in many things not in keeping with the tenets of Christianity. In 1573 the Council of the Marches in Wales expressed its concern over the number of alehouses in the country, where 'whoredom, filthy and detestable life much frequented, unlawful games as Tables, Dice, Cards, Bowls, Kayles [a form of nine-pin bowling], Quoits and such like commonly exercised'. Remarkably, it seemed that Tenby at this time had eighty alehouses to quench the thirst of a population estimated at 950! George Owen referred to various forms of recreation, including hunting, hawking, bowls and tennis – although technically the last two were prohibited because the authorities did not want the skills of archery neglected in case of war. Young people also enjoyed wrestling, throwing the stone and running.

ELIZABETHAN PEMBROKESHIRE

Elizabeth I's reign (1558–1603) has been called the golden age, with its economic prosperity, exploration of new lands, scientific and technological advances and cultural renaissance. In the context of Wales, the publication of William Morgan's translation of the Bible into Welsh in 1588 remains a milestone in literary and religious achievements, dedicated to Elizabeth I, who had commissioned it. All the churches in Pembrokeshire and the rest of Wales were meant to have a copy, with the aim of bringing the Church and scriptures closer to the people. According to the National Trust, there are only twenty-four known copies remaining, one of which is available in St Davids Cathedral Library among its 7,000 books, in a collection dating back to the 1500s.

Wales and Pembrokeshire featured in the works of the world's best-selling playwright. In particular, Shakespeare's romance *Cymbeline* is set largely in West Wales. Imogen, the play's heroine, asks how far it is to 'blessed Milford', where she is set to meet her lover Posthumus. Part of the plot revolves around her getting lost in the mountainous countryside. Despite the invitation to explain 'how Wales was made so happy as to inherit such a haven', literary critics suggest that Milford represented a focal point for anxieties, given that it was seen as a likely entry route for any Spanish invasion. According to George Owen, Milford was the most famous port in Christendom. In his own survey of the haven, he reported sixteen creeks, five bays and thirteen roads, although the latter were more like trackways.

Notwithstanding the tensions with Spain, Elizabethan Wales saw new exotic foods arriving in its ports. Tenby thrived in the sale of high-end goods. On 17 June 1566, the first cargo of oranges in Wales arrived at Tenby, offloaded from a Portuguese ship. We get a glimpse of what life was like in Tenby through the only surviving building of the period.

The Tudor Merchant House (Figure 15) is operated by the National Trust and furnished as it would have appeared 500 years ago. The Tudor reproduction furniture is made without glue or nails in the traditional way. The location on Bridge Street allowed easy access to the quayside and centre of town so that the owner could conduct business.

The ground floor was used as the merchant's shop and would have opened out into the street to drawn in passers-by. The merchant could sell goods straight from the ships, including wool, herbs, spices and sugar. Salt, imported from the Bay of Biscay, was highly prized for preserving meat and fish.

Archaeologists who examined the remains of the cesspit found evidence of fish and rats, parasites and eggshells. The house has Flemish-style chimneypieces on its three floors. There is also a fine fireplace. Firelight was supplemented by wax candles for those who could afford them, which were much brighter and clearer than cheaper tallow candles. Most cooking had to be done before dark.

The first floor was where the merchant and his family ate, lived and entertained visitors. A typical main meal taken before midday could contain four or five courses. The merchant and his wife slept on the second floor, which afforded a clear view down to the harbour to witness his ships coming and going. In the latrine tower is an explanation of how this worked. Clothes were hung above it in the belief that foul smells would kill fleas – the name 'garderobe' means private room, privy or lavatory.

Fig. 15 A bit of 'Old Tenby' featuring the Tudor Merchant's House. (*Thornhill-Timmins, 1895, pl. 13*)

A reconstructed Tudor trader's house, originally located in Quay Street, Haverfordwest, can also be seen at St Fagan's National Museum of History. The two-storeyed stone building has been refurbished to show what it may have looked like in 1580. The original owner was probably one of the town's prospering merchants. The cellar was used for storing grain, wool or other potential exports or imports such as wine, oil, soap or fruit, while the upper floor was either rented to a tenant or another trader.

From the mid-sixteenth century, Milford Haven was made the head port for south-west Wales. As a result, a series of official Port Books were introduced in 1559, offering valuable clues for historians on the nature of maritime trade. The customs officers were expected to record the dues to be collected, which were much needed by the Crown to meet the costs of war. The main imports into Pembrokeshire included French and Spanish wine, salt, oil, tar, fruit and luxury goods from as far afield as India, via Africa, Spain and Portugal. The exports were mainly wool, cloth, leather and timber, with small amounts of coal, which reflected the area's agricultural and industrial strengths.

For a coastal county such as Pembrokeshire, piracy was an endemic problem. It was made worse by the corruption and collusion of the local officials who were meant to uphold high standards of integrity, for example, in their roles as Justices of the Peace (JPs).

It was customary for squires to maintain their own small private army or band of retainers, composed of their own tenant farmers. Pembrokeshire historian Brian Howells described the dealings between the different factions as nothing less than 'small-scale private warfare'. He cites one vivid example when, in 1582, twenty of Sir John Perrot's men, armed with pitchforks and daggers, arrived at dawn in a field at Rhoscrowther. Their intention was to seize the crop grown by Griffith White of Henllan and hide it in Perrot's outbuildings. White spotted the group and tried to slash the traces (wagon straps) of the horses. In a scuffle, he was held on the ground at the point of a pitchfork and only rescued from injury by his sons. White, who was a JP, ordered the constable of the village, who was one of his own men, to call on his opponents to disperse in Queen Elizabeth's name while also alerting his own men to fire with bows and arrows if they failed to do so. Perrot's men duly fled.

Howard Lloyd, in his classic study of the gentry in south-west Wales between 1540 and 1640, observed that the difference between the gentry and the class below them was one of status and lineage rather than wealth. It was common for marriage to occur between the two groups and a yeoman could be materially better off than his gentleman neighbour.

Francis Jones, former archivist and author of *Historic Pembrokeshire Homes and Their Families*, pointed out that the Welsh gentry were far more numerous than those in England, but they had smaller estates and less grand houses. He traced more than 300 gentry residences in Pembrokeshire, although these were not from the same period. Most of these homes have disappeared or fallen into ruins.

The remains of Eastington Manor House (at Rhoscrowther), one of the properties belonging to the Perrot family, lies in the shadows of an oil refinery. The Coflein website (derived from the Welsh '*cof*', meaning memory, and '*lein*', meaning line), run by the Royal Commission on Ancient Historical Monuments in Wales, catalogues old monuments, including details and images of such houses.

It was not only the merchant classes who prospered during the Elizabethan era. As the great broadcaster Wynford Vaughan-Thomas put it, 'The average Elizabethan farmer was better clad. He and his peasants all had shoes, knitted stockings, jackets and felt hats.'

Ready money entered rural areas with the expansion of the cattle trade into the English markets. However, the authorities and those who were comfortable in life worried about the threat posed by vagrants who roamed about in bands, which is why punishments meted out to vagabonds were severe, with every parish having a whipping-post and stocks.

Poverty was endemic and made worse when harvests failed. Brian Howells points out that the poor were reduced to eating roots and bark. The passing of the Poor Law in 1601 aimed to provide relief for those in genuine need, including the aged, widowed and handicapped, while begging was outlawed.

8

THE CIVIL WARS,
1642–51

When James I became king in 1603, he inherited the broad support that the Welsh people had shown the Tudors. After all, James
was the great-great-grandson of Henry VII, and he was eager to
praise the Welsh for their loyalty and obedience. He made his son,
Henry, Prince of Wales in 1610.

James aimed to adopt a peacemaker role between the different
religious factions and he was well placed to do so. On the one
hand, he was baptised as a Catholic, the faith of his mother, Mary,
Queen of Scots. He also married Anne of Denmark, a Protestant,
who later converted to Catholicism. But James was actually raised
as a Presbyterian and remained a lifelong Protestant, commission-
ing the King James Bible, which appeared in 1611 and remains the
most popular translation in history.

James faced complex religious issues and had to contend with
growing dissatisfaction among the more extreme elements within
Protestantism. Puritans wanted to purify worship by stripping
away distractions and emphasising piety and the pursuit of values
such as hard work. They established footholds in towns such as
Haverfordwest and were to prove key players in the Civil Wars
that marred the reign of Charles I, the son and successor to James.

Most people in Pembrokeshire, particularly those living outside the main towns of Haverfordwest, Pembroke and Tenby, had
little stomach for civil war. They knew that the men they might
fight against were their neighbours and when hostilities ceased,
if they survived, would continue to be so. Pembrokeshire, and
Wales in general, lacked the middle classes of England, who were
more sensitive to the royal prerogatives impacting their estates,
while the appetite for Puritanism was not strong, at least before

1640. Nonetheless, traditional Pembrokeshire loyalty towards the monarchy meant that Charles I could count on a majority of pro-Royalist support among the gentry.

It was a complicated picture, with some gentry families switching allegiances for their own gain (for example, the Lort brothers of Stackpole and East Moor changed from Royalist to Parliamentarian). Others were reluctant to commit forces in either direction, while a few were ardent for their particular cause – for example, Sir John Stepney of Prendergast and the Catholic John Barlow of Slebech who supported the king, and Sir John Wogan of Wiston and Rice Powell, of Pembroke, who were behind the Parliamentarians.

At the heart of the Civil Wars was the deteriorating relationship between Parliament and the monarch over foreign policy, taxation and religious freedom, which culminated in the king's dismissal of Parliament in 1629. War with Scotland, and the need to pay for it, forced a return of Parliament in 1640. When Charles was presented with the Grand Remonstrance (1641), listing complaints about how he was running the country and his subsequent failure to arrest the Parliamentary leaders, war was on the cards.

In Pembrokeshire, the Parliamentarians soon took control of the fortified towns of Pembroke, Tenby and Haverfordwest. However, in 1643, both Tenby and Haverfordwest were captured by the Royalists. Pembroke held out and in subsequent years the toing and froing of fortunes for both sides meant that the outcome remained in the balance.

Sir Charles Gerard, a professional, hardened soldier, was sent by the king to take command of his forces and this appeared to turn the tide in his favour. In 1645, Gerard led a force of 2,500 men and inflicted heavy losses on Rowland Laugharne, who led the Parliamentarian troops. Gerard's withdrawal to England, where he was needed following the king's defeat at Naseby, allowed Laugharne to regroup and counter with a decisive victory at Colby Moor near Llawhaden. More than 750 of the king's men were captured and 150 killed. The remainder escaped to Carmarthen and when a royal garrison at Haverfordwest surrendered, Parliamentary victory was in sight.

By 1646, the Royalists had been defeated and Charles imprisoned. However, politically the country remained divided.

Parliament was mindful of the burden that higher taxation which was necessary for its New Model Army brought on the people and so moved to reduce this – in Pembrokeshire, the force was to be cut from 2,000 to 200 men. Laugharne and John Poyer, Pembrokeshire's Parliamentary military leaders, were against the proposals but faced their own problems. Both were summoned to Parliament to answer various accusations, including fraud, drunkenness and conspiring with Royalist agents. Then there were arguments over who should oversee Pembroke Castle and the disbanding of troops.

Encouraged by letters received from the exiled Prince Charles, Laugharne and Poyer switched allegiances and led the renewed Royalist cause, culminating in the Second Civil War of 1648. This hinged on the Battle of St Fagan's, where a force of 8,000 rebels outnumbered Parliament's New Model Army by more than two to one. However, the Parliamentarians held the advantage in terms of horses and several cavalry charges routed the Royalists.

Laugharne, Poyer and Powell retreated to Pembroke Castle, which was subsequently besieged by Oliver Cromwell's army. The arrival of heavy artillery signalled the end of the siege. Elsewhere, Cromwell's troops smashed the stained-glass windows and stripped the lead from St Davids Cathedral. They also burned books, ripped brasses from tombs and removed at least one bell. The cavalry were said to have left their hoofmarks on the cathedral floor.

The three captured Royalist leaders were convicted of treason and sentenced to death. On the basis of their former good service to Parliament and the fact that both Poyer and Laugharne had spent significant sums for the Parliamentary cause which they had not been compensated for, it was decided that two out of the three should be spared 'Life given by God'. A child was asked to draw lots and pulled out Poyer's name. Despite further remonstration, in 1649 Poyer was executed by firing squad in Covent Garden Market. Laugharne and Powell were eventually released and resumed their comfortable Pembrokeshire lives.

The Interregnum years, between the execution of Charles I in 1649 and the Restoration of his eldest son Charles II as monarch in 1660, were characterised by attempts to enforce a puritanical way of life. There followed what historian Geraint Jenkins called twenty years of 'blood and confusion'. Welsh Puritans such as John Penry sought to address the lack of spiritual leadership in the Church, thereby bringing people closer to God and away from the 'swarms of soothsayers and enchanters'.

The diocese had long struggled to counter superstition and religious doubt. In 1582, the Bishop of St Davids had warned that the preachers in his diocese were very poor and the people 'greatly infected' with atheism. And again in 1635, one of his successors lamented the lack of decent ministers to address and care for remote areas. Some parishioners had hardly ever heard a sermon, let alone one of decent quality.

By the time of the Civil Wars, the challenges of evangelising the dark corners of Pembrokeshire were clear. The lack of pamphlets in Welsh and the gentry's support for the king meant that the Puritan message of hard work, self-respect and higher duty to God (above their landowners) was hard to communicate. Although, under the Act for the Better Propagation and Preaching of the Gospel in Wales (1650), new schools were established in which children were taught to read their bibles, progress was hampered by the insistence that English was the language of instruction.

The Restoration of Charles II was generally welcomed by the people of Pembrokeshire, who found it difficult to live up to the expectations of a Puritan regime, which included banning Christmas because it was seen to encourage an immoral, profligate lifestyle. When Henry, the 1st Duke of Beaufort, visited Pembrokeshire in 1684 as the king's representative, he was greeted with fireworks and cheers of 'For God and the King'. Beyond the surface, however, there was probably a mix of apathy, pragmatism and self-preservation at work as people kept their heads down and went about their lives without any desire to attract the attention of the authorities. Neither the demise of the Stuarts nor the accession of George I as the first Hanoverian in 1715 sparked much of a reaction in Pembrokeshire, unlike in Scotland, where the Jacobite riots were in full swing.

9

EIGHTEENTH-CENTURY PEMBROKESHIRE

The eighteenth century saw major improvements in farming practices such as better crop rotation, more efficient ploughs and steam-powered machinery, all aspects of the Agricultural Revolution. The enclosure of open fields, through the erection of stone walls and fences and the planting of hedges, had actually begun in earlier centuries. This often proved controversial when it affected common land. In 1607, George Owen, for example, employed armed men to overlook the enclosure of land at Eglwyswrw and threatened to kill any commoners who got in the way. The enclosure of common and waste land, backed by Parliamentary legislation, was often followed by agricultural improvements, including drainage.

During the eighteenth century, the transport infrastructure was also improved by a network of roads managed by organisations known as Turnpike Trusts, who charged tolls for road maintenance. Better roads speeded up the movement of animals and crops.

These changes increased the supply of food to meet the needs of an expanding population. The growth of towns in England and South Wales meant more households to feed, clothe and keep warm, which increased demand for Pembrokeshire fish, beef, lamb, grain, wool and coal. This demand impacted the development of Pembroke and Milford as ports and boosted the overall local economy. In 1725, the famous author Daniel Defoe visited the county and was impressed by Pembroke, which he described as the largest and richest town in South Wales.

RICH AND POOR

Trade opportunities opened up and economic prosperity led to the birth of a 'consumer society' when more and more goods and services became affordable to ordinary families. This marked a shift from people looking to survive by meeting basic needs to fulfilling their desires – for example, in acquiring the latest fashionable clothing, food and household goods. Leading Pembrokeshire landowners, such as John Frederick Campbell, 1st Earl Cawdor of Stackpole Court, and Sir Richard Philipps, of Picton Castle, were among those who encouraged innovation to meet the growing economy.

Around 1800, the Brownslade Farm (now a listed building) on the Campbell estate in Castlemartin was leased to John Mirehouse, an 'agricultural improver', charged with developing a 'model' farm.

The country houses of the gentry – Picton Castle, Stackpole, Orielton, Colby House – were centres of social gaiety with balls, card parties and other entertainments. The diary of Sir John Philipps of 1757 describes a calendar of concerts, operas, dinner parties, whist games and other social engagements.

The gentry frequented highbrow balls held at the Assembly Rooms in Tenby and Haverfordwest. The local newspaper correspondent offered a veritable A–Z rollcall of the Pembrokeshire elite and among these are family names such as Allen, Leach, Bowen and Cawdor, which are still familiar in Pembrokeshire today.

Ladies were conveyed in their sedan chairs to these social functions. In the 1790s, the tourist Mary Morgan described how Pembrokeshire ladies did not in general display the style of the English ballroom dancers and was shocked at 'young folks with their hair down on their foreheads', who crowded together in a promiscuous manner at the top of the room. Meanwhile, 'those who are too polite, or too modest, to partake of the scramble, are thrust to the bottom'. Morgan was taken aback by the lack of restraint and the partying spirit of the young genteel women of Pembrokeshire, who followed the mantra:

Dance and sing, time's on the wing
Life never knows the return of Spring.

This was all great fun, but Morgan cautioned that in prolonging the spring they faced the prospect of 'a long and dreary winter'.

By the 1790s, the new fashions were for women to wear gowns that were classical in shape, slimmer, naturalistic and white or pale in colour. Sashes were tied around the waist and trains became fashionable, used mainly for evening wear. The 'in' fashion of the 1800s was to wear short-sleeved gowns and a short bodice with a low neckline and high waistline. Morgan thought that the Welsh female body shape 'has something of the Dutch roundness and plumpness' but conceded that Welsh women were very pretty, had delicate complexions and 'very fine teeth'. As for Welshmen, Morgan declared that they were 'remarkably handsome', and their strongest traits were hospitality, generosity and good humour.

This is the world of the novelist Jane Austen, who possibly visited Tenby around 1802. Touring Wales became a substitute for the 'Grand Tour' of Europe, which had been made difficult due to the war between the British and French. The surviving tourist diaries and guides offer a romantic, rose-tinted and rustic view of Pembrokeshire.

Fig. 16 Welsh beggar.
(*Louis Simond, 1815, p.211*)

In 1804, Benjamin Malkin praised the gentlemen of Pembrokeshire for furnishing labourers' cottages with necessary household articles at 'ordinary rates', in contrast to counties such as Carmarthen, Radnor and Glamorgan whose prices were the equivalent of major cities. He thought that the cottages were 'good and comfortable' and left Pembrokeshire cottagers the most contented in the land.

In reality, it is estimated that around one in five families throughout the country did not have enough money to feed, clothe, house themselves and keep warm. Begging was the only option for some people (Figure 16). As David Howell has shown, many families in eighteenth-century Pembrokeshire experienced grinding poverty and financial insecurity. Material relief occasionally came from benevolent gentlemen. For example, John Frederick Campbell paid for a whole ox and 100 loaves of bread to be distributed among the poor inhabitants of Tenby.

While widows, the elderly and children were most vulnerable to poverty, others slipped in and out of such a situation depending on their circumstances. A bad harvest, loss of work, sudden or prolonged illness – such factors meant that poverty was not always absolute.

LEISURE

While poverty was endemic, in the eighteenth century more and more people were enjoying better standards of living and material wealth. This was manifested in terms of pottery, furniture and clothing, as well as new cultural tastes such as the theatre, concerts, book shops, clubs, sport and other leisure pursuits. Much of this newfound wealth benefited seaside resorts such as Tenby, which could offer tourists health and leisure attractions as well as the scenery of sea, beach, rocks, cliff faces, piers, pavilions, boats, caves, inlets and small islands.

The rise of Tenby in the eighteenth century was part of Pembrokeshire's growing leisure industry. Guidebooks and tourist accounts made much of its landscape and pure air. Describing the beautiful views from hotel rooms became a key aspect of the genre.

John Jones, a medical man, promoted the health benefits of sea bathing in Tenby in 1781 and by the early nineteenth century, developments in the town were designed to make it a highly fashionable watering place. By 1811, there were two bathhouses and an assembly room paid for by Sir William Paxton. Bathing machines could be hired for those who wanted shelter and the service of a guide, for 1*s* 6*d*. However, it was still necessary to regulate the actions of bathers to preserve public decency. Mixed bathing was dismissed as a 'naughty French custom' and the rule was not relaxed until after the First World War.

RELIGION

The quest for the latest fashions and consumer goods was a world apart from the religiously minded, conservative voices that emphasised modesty, piety and other spiritual values in pursuit of long-term salvation rather than short-term hedonism. In the seventeenth and eighteenth centuries, Pembrokeshire had its Independent, Baptist and Quaker followings.

The Independent Albany Chapel in Haverfordwest was established as early as 1638. George Fox, the Quaker leader, arrived in Haverfordwest in 1657 and a meeting house was established in Haverfordwest (closed in 1829) and Milford (still open). The latter is said to have been built by the Nantucket whalers from Massachusetts, who founded Milford.

Methodism entered the county in the eighteenth century through the tours of major figures. Howell Harris from Breconshire inspired Howell Davies, 'the apostle of Pembrokeshire', to build a chapel at Woodstock in 1755. In the 1760s, Wesleyan Methodism was brought to Pembrokeshire by Thomas Taylor, a young Yorkshireman. Between 1763 and 1790, John Wesley himself made fourteen visits to the county. Both William Williams and Daniel Rowlands, the two leading Welsh Methodists, gave support and were hosted by George Bowen of Llwyngwair and the vicar of Newport.

Smaller religious groups were also active. The Moravians constructed their first chapel in 1773, although they were present in Haverfordwest from the 1740s and continued through until 1956. Branches were also established in Tenby and Pendine.

By the mid-nineteenth century, Pembrokeshire's main religious adherents were Baptists, Calvinistic Methodists (Presbyterians) and Independents (Congregationalists). Despite their differences with the Anglican Church, they shared a belief in the importance of a Bible-based education as the route to salvation.

SCHOOLING THE POOR

The religiously minded were among those who made concerted efforts to provide a basic schooling for the poor. Mary Tasker of Rudbaxton (who died in 1685) endowed a school 'for the breeding and maintenance of poor children of both sexes between the ages of nine and thirteen years who should be apprenticed to convenient trades'. In 1706, an adjoining almshouse and school were built in Haverfordwest. The boys must have been quite a sight in their uniform of long-tailed blue coats, turned up with scarlet-red waistcoats with brass buttons, corduroy knee breeches, grey worsted stockings and buckled shoes.

Sir John Philipps of Picton Castle was the key patron behind the Society for the Promotion of Christian Knowledge (SPCK), a charity set up in 1698 to provide schools for the poor. He founded seventeen out of thirty-one SPCK schools in Pembrokeshire, as well as supporting missionary activity abroad and the building of churches in London. Philipps was very hands-on in his approach, visiting schools to offer commendation and suggesting how they could improve. He also believed that the wives and daughters of the gentry had a role to play in 'making Caps, Kerchiefs, Aprons, Bands, and even Shirts for the poor', including a wish that his own daughter 'busy her[self] in making some provision for the Charity children'.

These efforts were surpassed by Philipps's brother-in-law, the remarkable Griffith Jones. He was rector of Llanddowror (in Carmarthenshire), who, in the 1730s, established a highly successful circulating school movement. The simple idea was for travelling teachers to spend a few months teaching children and adults to read the Bible in their own Welsh language using church vestries or whatever building was available, before moving to the next community. It is estimated that 250,000 individuals in Wales became literate as a result, although Jones had to fend off critics, who were anxious that an educated poor would gain ideas above their station in life.

Such fears were not unfounded as food riots were common throughout the century, particularly during years of scarcity and high prices. In 1740, for example, colliers boarded a vessel at Pembroke and stole corn that was about to be exported. In the 1790s, food riots took place in Narberth, St Davids, Pembroke and Haverfordwest.

Political upheaval in Ireland forced well-to-do Irish families to cross the Irish Sea to escape revolutionaries. Paul O'Leary, who has written about Irish immigration in Wales, estimates that around 2,000 Irish landed in Pembrokeshire in 1798 alone. The episode illustrates how migration was not limited to the next generation of Irish poor devastated by the Great Famine.

10

VICTORIAN AND EDWARDIAN PEMBROKESHIRE

QUEEN VICTORIA'S REIGN

Queen Victoria's long reign between 1837 and 1901 witnessed major technological and social changes, although the pace of change was slower in Pembrokeshire than the more urbanised counties of South Wales. Nonetheless, an elderly person looking back on New Year's Eve in 1900, whether in Tenby, Haverfordwest or Fishguard, must have reflected on a century of huge change.

In 1910, 105-year-old Hannah Rowlands explained eloquently to a newspaper reporter how 'towns and villages have sprung up with great rapidity, while new industries have been established in quick succession'. She had lived in Pembroke for ninety-six years but remembered Cardiff and Swansea as 'overgrown villages'.

Ten years into her reign, Victoria visited Pembrokeshire. In August 1847, the royal party undertook a yachting cruise from Osborne House on the Isle of Wight to the west coast of Scotland, which called for a stopover at Milford Haven to take in coal.

On 14 August, the *Victoria and Albert* arrived at the same spot that George IV had anchored in 1821 on his way to Ireland. The plans were for a guard of honour to receive the queen on the marine depot with a royal salute from the adjacent fortifications. The Earl of Cawdor placed his Stackpole mansion at Victoria's disposal. Excitement in Pembroke mounted. Every room was taken at the aptly named Victoria Inn, which opened in 1837 when the princess succeeded to the throne, while all private lodging houses in the district were fully booked.

It must have been a major disappointment when Victoria did not disembark to meet the crowds. In her journal, which can be read online, she records feeling seasick in the early morning.[3] By 5 p.m. she felt well enough to take a barge across Milford Harbour. Prince Albert was taken ashore to Pembroke Dock, accompanied by Lord Cawdor and naval officers, to inspect the garrison before proceeding to Bush Hill to get a good view of the surroundings. The *Pembrokeshire Herald*, the first Pembrokeshire-based newspaper issued in 1844, sympathised with those who waited all day for the queen to make an appearance.

From the royal yacht, Victoria produced a watercolour of Milford. Numerous boats came out to see the yacht, 'with Welsh women in their curious high-crowned men's hats'. Sir Richard Phillips of Picton Castle presented the queen with a gift of ripe fruits. Victoria, donning her white straw bonnet with a light blue feather and wearing a dark gown, acknowledged the welcome that she received. Those fortunate to catch sight of Victoria must have been taken aback by her diminutive stature – she was only 1.52m (just under 5ft), which journalists conceded was far shorter than they thought. A hundred seamen on board wore white uniforms and blue turned-down collar immaculately, while the fiddle and tambourine played through the evening.

When the word 'Victorian' is mentioned today, it usually conjures up images of strait-laced, prudish figures who valued such things as self-discipline, respect for their elders, punctuality and 'Godliness'. Victorian society was far more diverse, colourful and vibrant than this. The writer Matthew Sweet points out, for example, that most of the pleasures we take for granted originated with the Victorians. They invented the theme park, the shopping mall, the movies, organised sports such as football and rugby, the amusement arcade, cycling, photography, home shopping by mail order, comics, the crime novel and sensational newspaper stories.

Railways

Perhaps the greatest symbol of the Victorian age was the steam engine. The earliest rail travellers heading into West Wales could

---

3   http://www.queenvictoriasjournals.org/quick/executeSearch.do

take a train from Paddington to Bristol and then continue westwards by sea or take the South Wales Railway from Chepstow to Swansea, which opened in 1850. In 1853, the railway reached Carmarthen and a coach then took passengers further west. The opening of stations at Narberth Road, Clunderwen (1854) and then Neyland (1859) shortened the journey. In 1863, the Pembroke & Tenby Railway opened, with passengers crossing by ferry from Neyland (New Milford) to Pembroke Dock. The line was extended to Whitland by 1868, where it joined the South Wales Railway main line.

The tourist Philip Henry Gosse provides a rare glimpse of what it was like to travel by rail to West Wales in the earliest days (Figure 17). Peering out from the carriage on his way to Tenby in 1854, he describes passing the Swansea Copperworks bellowing out its 'thick yellow masses from the shafts of the smelting furnaces'. This 'pall of death' faded as he approached the beautiful Bay of Carmarthen. Two of his fellow passengers, young Welsh mechanics 'munching enormous flat cakes', offered a commentary on the sights they passed before alighting at Ferryside. Gosse and his family continued on their journey before the guard ran along the train shouting, 'Narberth Road and Tenby!', which forced a rather hurried scene of snatched umbrellas, coats and carpetbags.

It took seven hours to travel from London to Narberth Station. Gosse's anxiety over how to reach his final hotel accommodation

STARTING FROM	WEEK DAYS.				SUNDAYS.			
	1 & 2 class	1 2 3 class	Expr. 1 & 2	Mail 1 & 2	1 2 3 class	1 2 3 class	Mail 1 & 2	
	a. m.	a. m.	a. m.	p. m.	p. m.	p. m.	a. m.	
Paddington......	..	..	9 40	8 55	..	..	8 55	
Glo'ster	..	6 30	12 30	1 15	..	..	1 15	
Cardiff..........	6 25	8 42	2 6	3 55	..	4 48	3 55	
Swansea	8 30	10 50	3 40	5 40	7 15	7 10	5 40	
Carmarthen	9 52	12 35	4 35	7 5	8 37	8 52	7 5	
Narberth Road...	10 40	1 38	5 31	7 45	9 29	9 44	7 45	
	Expr. 1 & 2	1 2 3 class	Mail 1 & 2	1 2 3 class	1 2 3 class	Mail 1 & 2	1 2 3 class	
	a. m.	p. m.	p. m.	p. m.	a. m.	p m.	p. m.	
Narberth Road...	9 47	1 40	5 0	7 8	9 35	5 0	5 35	
Carmarthen	10 39	2 40	5 45	8 10	10 35	5 45	6 35	
Swansea	11 55	4 10	7 0	9 34	12 5	7 0	8 5	
Cardiff..........	1 4	6 27	8 35	..	3 3	8 35	10 16	
Glo'ster	2 30	8 43	11 0	..	5 16	11 0	..	
Paddington......	6 0	..	4 15	..	10 0	4 15	..	

Arrivals and Departures at Narberth Road Station.   SOUTH WALES RAILWAY.

Fig. 17 South Wales Railway timetable. (*Tenby Observer, 21 July 1854*)

was relieved by the sight of coachmen vying for his custom to take his party to one of Tenby's two hotels:

> Their intense earnestness and rivalry were most laughable 'Coburg, Sir?', 'White Lion, sir?', 'This is the coach for Tenby, sir;' 'the Coburg, sir!'; 'Here you are, sir'; 'for Tenby sir'; 'This the best coach sir'; 'Take your little gentlemen for half-price sir! Four shillings each, and only two for him!'; 'You shall go to the White Lion, sir, for three shillings a-piece!'

Despite the competition, as it happened, the eighteen or so passengers ended up equally divided among the two coachmen as they sped on their way. Gosse relates how the villagers came out to watch the Tenby coaches pass through, including Welsh women donning their 'dark-blue hose and petticoat, white flannel shawl, or red and yellow handkerchief, cap and pink ribbons surmounting by an immense black beaver hat'. A keen naturalist, Gosse enjoyed the roadside hedgerows full of honeysuckle, foxgloves, dog roses and campions, and the impressive overhanging oak trees. It was clearly a pleasant relief from the confines of the rail carriage. When they finally arrived at the Coburg Hotel, Gosse was refreshed by a cup of tea before venturing out for an evening stroll across to St Catherine's Island to explore the caves.

Not everyone welcomed the railways. Granted, they provided Pembrokeshire farmers with speedier access to markets in England and the growing urban demand for milk. Equally, however, foreign producers could more easily transport their produce around England and Wales. Well-to-do landowners and tenants also expressed concerns over the nuisance caused by railways cutting across their lands. David Howell cites both the Picton and Slebech estate owners as examples, the latter conceding that he might allow the line but only if he retained the right to halt the train 'on the spot in question on a given signal being given'.

Stagecoach operators also worried over the impact the railway would have on their respective businesses. Still, the coming of the railways brought new business to West Wales, such as the newsagent W.H. Smith (named after William Henry Smith), whose presence in Pembrokeshire began with a news stand at Haverfordwest Station before a shop was opened in Salutation Square in 1905.

The Industrial Revolution

The basis for far-reaching change in Victorian society was the Industrial Revolution, which began in the late eighteenth century. The notion of revolution suggests a dramatic change, although it was, in fact, a gradual process of social and economic transformation, arising from the basic commercial desire to make more money by harnessing technologies and efficient working practices. The changes were literally fuelled by 'black gold' and the prosperity brought by the coal mining industry. Crafts ranging from brewing to brickmaking needed hotter temperatures than could be afforded through the burning of wood.

Coal production improved with the introduction of steam-powered technology to pump out the water that regularly flooded the mines. Coke or coal residue powered the ironworks and factory machinery, which produced goods for both the domestic and global markets. By the 1850s, Britain became known as 'the workshop of the world', with the South Wales mining valleys very much at its centre.

Pembrokeshire had its own, much smaller coalfield of high-quality anthracite. What made the coal special was its smoke-free heating qualities. It was widely regarded as among the best coal in the world. Coal had been mined in Pembrokeshire as early as the 1330s.

So many pits had opened in Begelly in the sixteenth century that there were fears that the main road running through the village might collapse with subsidence, leaving carriage drivers reluctant to pass through. By the 1800s, Pembrokeshire had around sixty or so mines and pits, providing employment to more than 1,000 men and women. The women serviced the equipment or were engaged in winding coal and filling carts (Figure 18).

Captain Child, one of the owners of Begelly Colliery, suggested that the women worked harder than the slaves in the West Indies, but added, 'There was an absence of better employment in the district'. According to one miners' agent, children were employed 'as soon as they can stand on their legs' as air-door keepers. Five- and six-year-olds sat beside an air-door and opened it for the haulier with his horse and tram to pass through. Robert Franks, an inspector of mines, summed up their circumstance, 'With his solitary candle, cramped with cold and wet and not half fed, the pit child, deprived of light and air, passes his silent day.'

At Broadmoor Colliery, officially the boys started work at the age of 7 and girls at the age of 12. They typically worked for eight to ten hours a day with Sundays as a day of rest.

At Kilgetty Colliery, boys operated in the tightest of spaces, less than 3ft 6in in height and 3ft width. In 1842, Elias Jones, aged 14, explained, 'It is very hard work, indeed it is too hard for such lads as we, for we work like little horses'. Jones had pulled carts underground since the age of 8.

Boy guiding skip down an incline of 45⁰ See Diag 2.

Windlass girls and coal wheelers in Pembrokeshire.

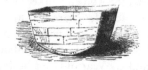

Sectional view of Diag. 1 with girls winding coal from the workings in the dip.

Fig. 18 Pembrokeshire miners.
(*Report of the Children's Employment Commission*, 1842)

The incentive was that the more they carted, the more they earned, but as a drained 13-year-old Ann David put it, 'The time is long, and the work very hard indeed [...] sad tiring sort, and I feel very glad when over'.

James Bowen, the Narberth surgeon, put it as diplomatically as he could when he explained that the 'practice of taking children down the mines at the present early age has a manifest tendency to shorten the average duration of human life'.

Parents were driven by poverty to send their youngsters below ground. The agent for the Landshipping Colliery justified the employment of young children simply because there was no machinery that could do the work instead. The colliery was abandoned in 1845 following the drowning of forty-five miners, including children.

While families needed the income from their children's labour, the growing humanitarian influence of social reformers began to play on the conscience of politicians, the landowning classes and the general public. Coal mining was dangerous work and posed serious health hazards. Deaths and serious injuries were common. Colliers suffered bronchitis and respiratory problems. The average life of a collier was 40 and only a handful exceeded the age of 60.

There were dangers brought by flooding, fire, damp, collapsed roofs, gas poisoning and faulty equipment. In 1844, seven miners were killed at Begelly when the chain broke on their tub. In 1847, 13-year-old Martha John and two boys fell to their deaths in the shaft at Moreton Colliery as they were transported down to the pit floor.

The greatest loss of life in Pembrokeshire occurred in 1844 when forty miners drowned as sea water burst through Garden Pit. Part of the mine actually ran below the East Cleddau Estuary, and it flooded within minutes. In 2002, a memorial plaque was erected and then rededicated in 2019 when further research revealed the identities of the missing names. Researchers reckon that the person originally listed as 'child' was almost certainly Joseph Harts, aged 4. Seven out of the forty victims were aged 10 or under.

Even the morning journey to the pits could prove challenging. Mary Thomas fell into a flooded pit shaft and drowned, while the same fate befell Thomas Smith when he slipped on his way to work at Begelly, falling into a disused pit. One of the problems was that when the coalpits had been worked out, in time they became overgrown with weeds and brambles, which meant that the unwary could easily succumb to a fatal stumble.

Many children walked to the pits in nothing but rags to cover their feet. In his study of the Pembrokeshire coalfield, Martin Connop-Price explains that during winter the rags would freeze to the ground and the boys had little choice but to urinate on their own feet to free them.

Once underground, the boys worked barefoot, wearing a shirt and pants. Eight-year-old Benjamin Thomas, whose father had died, worked barefoot with his sister, three brothers and mother in the pit. He was described by the visiting assistant commissioner as 'a very pitiful-looking little fellow'.

Tom Waters recalled working at Kilgetty in the 1890s when the sharp anthracite coal would cut his feet and when he returned home, his father used hot tallow candle wax to prise out the coal from their skin. Affordable boots were not commonly worn until the twentieth century, and even then, they were often kept for 'Sunday best' and attending chapel. On the pit surface, women sought to protect their faces and hair from the coal dust by tying scarves around their heads, down to their chins.

But it was not only the physical dangers posed to children working underground. For the Victorians, the pits also exposed children to moral corruption as they mingled with miners who drank, smoked and swore. It didn't matter that these were their fathers, brothers, uncles and neighbours.

Legislation was passed in 1842 banning women and children under the age of 10 from working underground. However, enforcement was difficult because of a shortage of inspectors and so the practice continued. As late as the 1890s, at least one woman recalled working underground in the Kilgetty pit when asked, only staying at home on full pay when notice was received of a visit from the mines inspector.

Schooling

In 1833, the state introduced grants to support two societies who led the way in providing elementary schooling for the poor: the

National Society, run by Anglican Church, and the non-denominational British and Foreign School Society. Despite the success of the Sunday schools, there was a general consensus that more needed to be done to teach children how to read and other basic skills, as well as how to behave themselves and respect authority.

This was reinforced by the infamous 1847 report on the state of education in Wales. The commissioners pulled no punches in portraying low-quality teaching and learning, inadequate resources and irregular attendance – just under 50 per cent of Pembrokeshire children attended school for less than a year. The commissioners and their assistants were impressed with only a handful of schools in the county.

At Lamphey, for example, boys were seen to be making excellent maps of the Holy Land, the copybooks of the senior classes were very well written, the reading of the fifth chapter of Daniel was remarkably good and the children could give a good account of the story of Moses. This example illustrates the narrowness of the curriculum and the religious frame of mind upon which educational success was often judged. The following extracts give a broader flavour of the state of education and perceived moral standards in mid-Victorian Pembrokeshire:

Village school [at Wiston] [...] the room is little better than a mud hovel – dark and meanly furnished with tattered books lying about.

Parish of Claberston [...] labourers in the parish were wretchedly poor and unable to send their children to school if they had to pay for it. The cottage I was in was a wretchedly dirty place. The pig was walking about the house as if one of the inmates. I saw six children; they appeared [...] as wild as possible.

Dewisland [...] the unmarried man-servants in the farms range the country at night; and it is a known and tolerated practice, that they are admitted by the women-servants at the houses to which they come. I heard the most revolting anecdotes of the gross and almost bestial indelicacy with which sexual intercourse takes place on these occasions.

It was such remarks on the people's immorality and character which overshadowed what was a relatively accurate picture of educational poverty in Pembrokeshire and most other parts of England and Wales.

The report conveyed a very different world to that presented in the Great Exhibition held in London's Hyde Park a few years later. The *Pembrokeshire Herald* reported the excitement of the wave of visitors when the exhibition doors opened to the public on 1 May 1851. It meant, however, that the Milford Regatta had to be cancelled, owing to 'the superior attractions afforded by the Great Exhibition'. It was a truly educational experience, with 15,000 exhibitors from forty foreign countries and 10 miles of frontage for the display of goods. Visitors were enthralled by the exotic, including Indian silks alongside a huge stuffed elephant, Chinese porcelain, watches from Switzerland and French tapestries. The best of British industrial and technological progress was arranged in thirty categories. Of particular relevance to Pembrokeshire, new agricultural innovations boasted everything from straw shakers to turnip cutters. Civil engineering displayed huge lighthouse lenses to demonstrate the latest construction techniques. In the words of the historian Asa Briggs, this was the 'age of things'.

Poverty

Of course, many of the things on display at the Great Exhibition were well beyond the financial reach of ordinary families. It was an age of two nations. Propping up society were those variously described as tramps, vagabonds, vagrants and beggars. These terms were often used interchangeably. Technically, tramps were homeless people who did not necessarily beg, while vagabonds were literally those who wandered the countryside (from the Latin '*vagari*', to wander). The Elizabethan Laws introduced the term 'rogue' to describe anyone who had no land, no master and no legitimate trade or source of income.

In 1795, magistrates in the village of Speenhamland (Berkshire) introduced a system of means-tested wage supplements to help the rural poor cope with high grain prices following a series of bad harvests. Although well intentioned and popular in some counties, it was not adopted nationally. One of the criticisms was that employers then paid below subsistence wages, knowing that the difference would be made up by parish rates.

The desperate might turn to acts of charity. The Church was obliged to offer the poor food, material goods or money in the form of 'alms' (from Old English '*ælmysse*', meaning 'pity' or 'mercy' in Greek). An extension of this led to the setting up of almshouses, supported by various charities and individuals. For example, funds from the Perrot Trust, named after the benefactor Sir John Perrot, built a row twelve houses in Barn Street, Haverfordwest, which operated as almshouses between 1846 and 1866. Fresh Beach Cottage in Castlemartin is now a holiday let but was once an almshouse built in 1870 by Lord Cawdor to accommodate the poor. In the north-west corner of St Mary's Churchyard in Carew is Alms Row, where another nineteenth-century almshouse stands.

Hunger and the fear of it continually vexed many families in the nineteenth century. The so-called 'Hungry Forties', witnessed by a slump in trade, leading to high unemployment, coupled with a bad harvest, proved a miserable time for the poor. Cases were brought before the Pembrokeshire courts of women stealing milk, turnips or whatever food they could find. In 1847, Elizabeth Evans, a 30-year-old servant from Pembroke, was convicted of stealing one loaf of barley bread and one pint of milk. Frances Evans, probably her sister, was also charged with receiving the said loaf and milk, 'knowing them to have been stolen'. Frances also had a child, but this made no difference in lightening the sentencing – both sisters were sent to Haverfordwest gaol to serve a month's hard labour. This meant walking a treadmill in small groups for ten-hour shifts. The authorities saw this as productive punishment – the wheel turned a millstone which ground the corn for the prison bread.

Families could find that their plight worsened overnight for all kinds of reasons such as a bout of unemployment, a workplace accident, a run of poor harvests, illness, bad luck or misdemeanours committed by a family member. In 1843, a well-respected Pembrokeshire farmer was fined a shilling because his 15-year-old son, one of nine children, engaged in a game of potato-throwing and a potato struck a female labourer. She took the matter to the local magistrate and the case ended up in court. Even though the magistrate had his doubts, he was overruled by the bench of four and the fine was issued along with a crippling 9s in costs. As the doubtful magistrate explained, the boy 'had not 6d. in the world; and his father, having a wife and eight young children to maintain, was obliged to pay that'.

Most authorities took for granted the universality of the stable two-parent family dependent largely on the father's wage. If unemployment occurred, this was viewed as voluntary, temporary and curable through self-help and an expanding economy. However, it was recognised that among the poor were those deserving of support, such as the sick, insane, elderly, orphans and widows. One can only imagine the heartache of the mother who, in 1856, left her new-born son in a basket in the passageway of the Blue Boar Inn in Haverfordwest, accompanied by a note: 'Pleas to be as kind as to call this child Edwin, that he is requested'.

It was common to send children out to work by the age of 10, initially running errands or fetching things, 'progressing' to heavier and life-threatening work in the fields and pits. Mothers might also try to eke out a living through some form of homework or would seek employment, leaving the care of the youngest children to relatives, neighbours or older children.

Those children who were unfortunate enough to lose both parents were sent to the workhouse and faced the prospect of further emotional trauma. The concept of the workhouse was straightforward. Those who were unable to support themselves and their families were provided with accommodation and food in exchange for work.

Parish workhouses had been established in the 1770s (for example, at St Florence, Manorbier and Pembroke). Mass unemployment following the end of the Napoleonic Wars in 1815 and a series of poor harvests put considerable strain on the system. Law of 1834 aimed to discourage relief to any who refused to enter workhouses, managed by newly established Poor Law Unions on the principle that those in the workhouse were not meant to be better off than those hard-working people on the outside.

Most adult paupers who were able bodied received 'outdoor relief', assistance in the form of money, food or clothing. Those who did enter the workhouse were categorised as 'inmates', language which effectively equated them with criminals. In short, the work-house was associated with the 'mad, bad and dangerous to know'.

Workhouses soon became symbols of shame and conflict. In January 1839, special constables were needed to protect the build-ing of a new workhouse at Narberth after a mob attempted to burn it down as part of the Rebecca Riots (1839–43). This was a protest movement in West Wales composed mainly of agricultural labourers and farmers who had been angered over the cost and frequency of road tolls, among other issues.

On 13 May 1839, agricultural labourer Thomas Rees, who acquired the nickname 'Twm Carnabwth' (Tom Stone Cottage), was one of the ringleaders who orchestrated an attack on the Efailwen Tollgate, in Carmarthenshire, which represented the oppressive system. Rees lived in his one-room cottage, 20ft by 12ft, with his wife Rachel and their three children. He was a colourful character, 'game for anything', as historian Pat Molloy puts it.

Rees was a talented man. He was the chief reciter of the catechism (*Pwnc*) in his local chapel at Mynachlog-ddu, a prize-winning boxer, which cost him the sight of one eye, and the local leader of the *Ceffyl Pren* (literally, 'wooden horse') custom of imposing rough justice. Fathers of bastard children, who aban-doned their responsibility, adulterers and harsh landlords were examples of those who had offended the strong rural sense of morality. They were subjected to a mock trial and then carried backwards through the village on a ladder or pole to the scorn of villagers dressed in women's clothes and with painted faces, sym-bolising a crooked world.

It was a small step to channel the aggression and boisterous nature of the *Ceffyl Pren* towards other targets. One tale has it that the stature of Tom Rees meant that only one woman had a petticoat big enough for him to wear – an old maid called Rebecca, who lived in the neighbouring parish of Llangolman. And this exchange, so the story goes, was the basis of the name Rebecca Riots. However, it is more likely the case that the movement was named after a biblical verse (Genesis 24:60) that was familiar to Thomas Rees and was taken as God's blessing to 'possess the gates of their enemies'. Surprisingly, given his role in the riots, there is no mention of this on his gravestone at Bethel Chapel at Mynachlog-ddu. Instead, the inscription, roughly translated to

English, reads: 'No one but God know what may happen in a day. While fetching a cabbage for my dinner, death came to my garden and struck me.'

As economic conditions deteriorated, in 1843 the authorities received threatening notices that unless the paupers received better food, the workhouse would be attacked. This prompted the clerk of the Poor Law Union to publish in the press a statement of unqualified support for the workhouse management. For reassurance, the Castlemartin Yeomanry were deployed to keep the peace.

The authorities persisted with the line that workhouses should be run on the principle of economy, given that the buildings were funded by ratepayers. This parsimonious spirit persisted well into the twentieth century. Historian Roger Turvey points out that as late as 1924, the Narberth guardians turned down a decision to install electricity because it was 'the wrong time for luxuries'.

The stigmatising of the poor was a question often debated by the Pembrokeshire Boards of Guardians, who ran the workhouses. At a meeting in 1873, the Haverfordwest Guardians argued over whether pauper names should be published more regularly in the newspapers. The general practice was for Poor Law Unions to publish the list of their paupers twice a year. Supporters pointed to cases of paupers taking payments of outdoor relief and then heading off to work in Merthyr earning full pay. This was not in the ratepayers' interests. Publishing the names of paupers, it was reasoned, would heighten awareness in the community of potential abuses and help officials (relieving officers) in their enquiries. Others argued that this would be insensitive and only bring shame to paupers and their families.

The Census returns identify by name those who had fallen on hard times. For example, the 1881 Census for Haverfordwest Workhouse lists children of the Cambridge family – James, aged 12, Mary, aged 10 and John, aged 8, from Llanycharn. They may have been orphans or perhaps their parents had abandoned them. Also in the workhouse was Fanny Anthony, a 41-year-old charwoman from Milford Haven with her three children, aged 12, 9 and 2. Of the 148 inmates, more than a third were aged 10 or under.

The elderly were also present in workhouses. In 1901, Thomas Philpin was the oldest pauper at the Pembroke Workhouse. He was born in Rhosmarket in 1797, shortly after the Fishguard Invasion.

He was the son of a poor farmer, who recalled a diet consisting of little more than barley bread. In 1898, *The Cardiff Times* described him as 'a son of the soil, a typical specimen of the class'. His work-house pleasures included an allowance of one ounce of tobacco.

Despite the monotony endured by the likes of Philpin, work-houses did provide food, shelter and a modicum of comfort which could not be found on the outside. Moreover, children received a basic schooling in reading, writing and arithmetic, and sometimes vocational skills such as sewing for girls. The schooling was gener-ally of a low standard, but at least this was better than the majority of their peers outside the workhouse who did not attend any school.

While it is common for historians to focus on those sent to the workhouses and the reported abuses, it is also worth sparing a thought for the staff. They often faced challenging conditions, were generally disliked and poorly paid. Many medical officers were young and lacked experience, while female staff sometimes ran the risk of inappropriate advances from male colleagues. In 1908, a nurse named Wragg made a formal complaint of assault against Charles Flutter, the master of the Pembroke Workhouse. Although an investigation cleared Flutter of impropriety, when his wife resigned as matron due to ill health, the Guardians decided not to renew his contract.

Not everyone was moved by the plight of the poor, especially those who were considered undeserving of help. In 1885, one Haverfordwest observer, 'an occupier of property truly disgusted in town', was appalled at the lack of gratitude among beggars. He cited examples of those who threw bread and other food that they received to the ground, demanding money instead, which 'they only wanted for drink'. But it wasn't only vagrants that troubled him. He took issue with unruly paupers who pestered houses and grocers in the High Street, engaged in drunkenness and fights and caused general levity and mischief in the town. Worse, there was not enough policemen to clear the streets.

Such social commentary was often a matter of perspective. For example, the contemporary American author Wirt Sikes had the impression that 'the strange and painful spectacles which so aston-ish foreigners in the streets of all large English towns, especially of women, staggering along with tottering legs and idiotic gaze, are very seldom seen in Wales'.

Health

The very poor, living in squalid cottages or no housing, lacking adequate diet and without the money for medicines and doctors, were the most vulnerable to disease and illness. Typhus, dysentery, typhoid and tuberculosis were all killer diseases.

Through the nineteenth century there were also regular outbreaks of cholera, spread by bacteria in contaminated water or food. The first recorded case in Pembrokeshire was in June 1832, although, as the *Carmarthen Journal* reported the following month, 'in order not to create an unnecessary alarm it has been kept secret'. In October, readers were informed that a crew member of a steamship had died of cholera and the body was brought to Milford. The ship was then ordered to be taken to sea, the body thrown overboard and the ship placed under quarantine.

In 1848, during the next major cholera outbreak, the Bishop of St Davids instructed the clergy to preach 'Temperance, Cleanliness and Ventilation', which were considered the three most important 'preservatives' from cholera. The 1848 Public Health Act led to the establishment of local boards of health and medical officers of health. However, one Tenby resident complained that such measures had little impact on the town where:

> ... persons are allowed to throw all sorts of vegetable refuse and garbage into the streets, where it lies putrefying for at least a week. Drains, instead of being kept free to run off, are choked up, and fill the air with noisome odours; and the back places are in a still worse condition. Pigsties remain uncleansed [...] Much unpleasant refuse is also thrown over the cliffs, which never reaches the bottom, and causes most offensive smells, and large rats congregate.

The Victorian mantra of 'cleanliness next to Godliness' was clearly easier to preach than put into practice.

In the 1850s, the writer William Thackery coined the phrase 'the great unwashed' and it was soon adopted to describe the appearance and smell of the working class. Although it was possible to buy from an apothecary dusting powders which absorbed sweat, it was only in the late nineteenth century that perfumed soaps (lavender, violet and rose) became popular and helped mask the sweat produced from long, arduous work.

As social historian Ruth Goodman points out, soap and hot water could prove substantial expenses for those living on or below the poverty line. Ordinary households simply could not afford to buy soap and so made their own out of wood ash and tallow, combined with limestone, but this was a tedious and time-consuming process.

In the 1830s, a 4oz bar of soap cost about the same as a good joint of beef. Although the tax on soap was abolished in 1853, in a family of five or six children, the cost of washing bodies and clothes with soap remained expensive. And yet, infrequent washing of clothes was not necessarily taken by social commentators as a sign of poverty. Housekeeping manuals advised that dirty linen should be accumulated and washed every three months or once a year. In large households, however, weekly washdays were necessary to process the amount of washing at hand, while washerwomen were often employed by those who could afford them.

It is important to bear in mind that most Victorian households did not have an indoor supply of piped water. Instead, water would be carried in pitchers or buckets from the nearest stream or well and stored in tubs or barrels. The strain of carrying buckets of water over some distance meant that a wooden yoke was often used to evenly balance the weight across the shoulders. Sometimes, it was easier to bring the soiled garments with the washtub to the stream to wash and rinse and then light a fire to dry the clothes. Rainwater was also gathered because its softness aided the lathering of clothes.

The Pembrokeshire newspapers frequently discussed the supply of water, which was a longstanding complaint. In 1909, housewives in Haverfordwest complained that they had no water with which to prepare meals.

The lack of clean water and basic sanitation contributed to a range of health problems. Although much is made of the cramped, overcrowded housing and the slums of nineteenth-century towns such as Swansea, Cardiff and Merthyr Tydfil, conditions in rural parts of Pembrokeshire were arguably worse. In 1905, the Medical Officer reported that in Fishguard, many residents went to the toilet in their gardens or fields and emptied household pails of excrement wherever they could. Householders also mixed their excrement with the ash from the fire and then dug this into the potato patch at the appropriate season. The most common privy, providing little privacy, consisted of an outhouse associated with a dump for waste (midden). Fishguard had only twenty-four of the more advanced water closets, leaving the town's Medical Officer to lament, 'Such conditions are hardly credible in these twentieth century days'.

Overcrowded housing aided the spread of infectious diseases and could have dire consequences. It was common for children to share beds. In 1907, the 3-day-old baby son of Martha and Thomas Allen, a baker from Haverfordwest, died when the infant was suffocated as he slept with his mother. When the coroner asked why the baby was in the bed, he was told there was nowhere else for him to sleep.

Bug infestations, poor hygiene and inadequate diet took their toll, particularly on the young. Children under the age of 5 accounted for four in every ten deaths in nineteenth-century England and Wales. Death was never far away, as the diary of David Williams, a self-employed carpenter from St Clears, revealed. Entries for 1882 and 1833 include: 'Will Soldier froze to death on the way home from Crymych'; 'George, Cwm Trelech, killed in a cart'; 'Will Gof died at 6'; and 'James, Castell Mawr, drowned in Lamb's winch'. In 1888, Williams recorded the death of his own daughter Rachel in the morning and attended her funeral in the afternoon.

Although the death of a child was a traumatic event, insurance companies suspected that there were those among the working classes who insured children 'for speculative and criminal purposes'. The House of Lords took this seriously enough to investigate the issue in 1891. Considerable money could be made from a child's death, leading to obvious temptations for poor parents. Children were enrolled in burial clubs, with a popular joke being, 'Aye, aye, that child will not live, it is in the burial club!' Legislation in 1896 reduced the amount that could be collected upon the death of a child.

For those seeking pain relief, drugs were widely available over the counter. They were not regulated until 1868, when sales were limited to registered chemists and pharmacies. Raw opium was often sold as pills, penny sticks or pennyworths – twenty or so drops for a penny. Opiates were appealing for both recreational and medicinal purposes because they were effective in reducing pain and there was general ignorance around their longer-term fatal consequences. Even so, readers of the *Pembrokeshire Herald* were warned that opium-takers find their 'eyes assume a wild brightness, the memory fails, the gait totters, mental exertion and moral courage sink, and a frightful marasmus or atrophy reduces the victim to a ghastly spectacle'.

In 1862, the dead body of the Reverend J.C. Sharpley from Tenby was discovered in his bedroom, with a bottle of opium found by the bedside. The inquest returned a verdict that he had died from taking Batty's Solution of Opium and Prussic Acid (hydrogen cyanide), in quantities not excessive but which, in his exhausted state of health, proved fatal.

Laudanum, the 'aspirin of the nineteenth century', was the most popular opium derivative. It comprised a tincture of opium mixed with wine or water. Opiates such as Godfrey's Cordial and Dalby's Carminative were deliberately given to children to keep them quiet while their mothers were at work. This was not limited to the working classes. As late as 1910, the *Evening Express* cited an article that the children of middle-class and well-to-do mothers were left drugged by sedatives given by 'ignorant' and 'lazy' nurses. In fact, these nurses usually operated under the housekeeper's instructions within a tight hierarchy of domestic servants. One 'fashionable' young mother explained:

My new nurse is a treasure. Baby never cries at night now. He sleeps without waking once. I am so thankful; it made us miserable to hear him cry. Oh, no, of course, I don't nurse him myself. What an idea! I can't give up my friends and my life for that.

Most households used laudanum as a painkiller for a wide range of ailments, including coughs, diarrhoea, 'women's troubles' and toothache.

Sugar was not considered a cause of tooth decay or other health problems. On the contrary, the *Pembrokeshire Herald* made it clear to its readers:

It is quite a mistaken idea to suppose that sugar injures the teeth. No persons have whiter teeth than the negroes, particularly during crop time [...] the more sugar is given to a child, the greater will be its health and strength.

In reality, even the wealthy who could afford the best dental care were likely to lose their teeth at some point. But at least they had the option of purchasing the latest dentures. At the most expensive end of the scale, teeth were made of walrus ivory fitted with silk ligatures and cost a hefty 10s. It was possible to buy human teeth, which had been removed from deceased criminals or soldiers. They were called 'Waterloo teeth', after the Battle of Waterloo in 1815 when teeth were scavenged from dead bodies on the battlefield. In extreme cases, paupers were also known to 'donate' their teeth for money.

In 1884, the Reverend Tomas Jones, the Wesleyan Minister at St Davids, was delighted with his new dentures, which arrived by post. Jones rejoiced, 'I am able to grind my food well and articulate properly.' His letter was part of an advertising campaign on behalf of the Swansea surgeon dentists, who offered clinics while visiting Tenby, Haverfordwest and Pembroke Dock.

Living Standards

Despite all the challenges relating to health and poverty, it is important to retain perspective. For most people, living standards gradually improved in the nineteenth century. More and more families enjoyed the recreational opportunities afforded by higher standards of living. The carpenter David Williams recorded going to the seaside with his family, enjoying the Crymych and Whitland Eisteddfodau, attending the St Clears Fair, brass band concerts and competitions, fishing and excursions, for example to Swansea.

A modern-day visitor taking a stroll around the county town of late-Victorian Haverfordwest would have been impressed by the range of shops and services available. There were saddlers, hatters, cork cutters, shoe and boot makers, glovers, jewellers, watchmakers, blacksmiths, butchers, grocers, furriers, tallow chandlers, hairdressers, tailors, tobacconists, banks, confectioners, chemists, photographic artists, a portrait painter and music teacher.

The skills of the local craftsmen were maintained through apprenticeship schemes and migration. The Dixons from Yorkshire, for example, came to the town in the 1860s and were highly skilled clog makers. There were around sixty bakehouses in the town and the likes of J. Davies & Son offered home delivery. A visitor to Haverfordwest at Christmas in 1884 marvelled at the range of cakes, jams, jellies, pickled fruits, cheeses and tinned meats available in the shops.

However, working-class families faced particularly difficult periods. The agricultural depression of the 1870s, following a series of poor harvests, forced rural workers to seek out higher wages in the industrial valleys of Glamorgan and Monmouthshire. Imports of American grain made possible by cheap transport left Welsh arable farmers struggling to stay afloat.

The sixty-four years of Victoria's reign were arguably the most transformational in the history of Pembrokeshire: from lighting by candlelight to the installation of electricity and gas (at least for those who could afford it); from horseback to rail travel; from ignorance to mass literacy, gained at a network of free elementary schools and, by the 1880s, new intermediate or secondary

ILFORD HAVEN TELEGRAPH JANUARY 23 1901

DEATH OF QUEEN VICTORIA.

HER MAJESTY'S LAST HOURS.

ROYAL FAMILY AT THE BEDSIDE.

Fig. 19 Death of Queen Victoria announced by the *Telegraph*. (*23 January 1901*)

schools; from impressions of the Pembrokeshire landscape based on artistic sketches to a precise photographic record; from sending messages via postboys on horses, which typically travelled at 3–4 miles per hour, to almost instant delivery via telegrams.

Indeed, it was a telegram that carried the news of Victoria's death on 22 January 1901. The *Telegraph* reported that there was 'a stampede of the Pressmen' outside the gates of Osborne House on the Isle of Wight when the queen's death was announced at 6.30 p.m., each anxious to be the first to send the news across the country:

> Some rushed to conveyances which they had in waiting, others despatched bicyclists, who hurried as fast as wheels could carry them to the telegram office at East Cowes. One or two started off on full gallop.

Within thirty or so minutes, a notice was placed in the window of Miss John, a bookseller in Haverfordwest. No wonder the telegraph has been dubbed the Victorian internet.

Victoria's end cast a shadow of collective grief across Pembrokeshire for what one Milford magistrate called the death of 'their Mother Queen'. The Chairman of Pembrokeshire County Council described her as 'the noblest, purest, wisest and best Sovereign'. Church bells in the town were also rung and the flag flown at half-mast. On the following day, the newspaper columns were edged in black and conveyed with appropriate solemnity details that had been released of Victoria's final moments (Figure 19). Throughout the county, events were postponed, from the fire brigade's annual tea and dance to the Pembrokeshire Hounds meeting.

EDWARDIAN PEMBROKESHIRE

As the new Edwardian era began, three national issues impacted the people of Pembrokeshire. First, there did not appear to be an end in sight to the South African War (also known as the Boer War), which had started in 1899 with disputes between the Boer farmers and British over rights to diamond and gold deposits.

For West Wales, the war had personal meaning in the deployment of the Pembrokeshire Yeomanry alongside other Welsh soldiers. As they left Southampton, 'the men looked extremely fit and well, and with their brand new kharki [*sic*] uniforms, presented a very smart appearance,' reported the press. In fact, as a later inquiry revealed, many of the recruits were in poor physical condition, reflecting broader concerns about the health of the working classes.

The Pembrokeshire Yeomanry admitted that they were bored following their three-week training at Aldershot and could not wait to arrive at the Transvaal. However, such anticipation was soon tempered by the realities of scarce provisions, dust storms, below-freezing temperatures after dark, typhoid and a highly resolute and skilled opposition.

In April 1900, Trooper Evans from Burry Port (Carmarthenshire) wrote to his sister and confided how the Boers had everything built to suit them, with trenches, rock shelters and forts, coupled with knowledge of the landscape. He struggled to describe 'how it feels under fire, only that one loses all sense of fear'. One fellow rifleman alongside him was struck by a bullet through the wrist and, just as he exclaimed, 'Oh God, I am shot!', he was hit by another through the heart and fell dead.

Still, the press was keen to report how Evans's mood was lifted when he received the queen's chocolate tin box inscribed with the words, 'Wishing You a Happy New Year, Victoria'. Evans explained that locals had already offered him £5 for it but he reassured his sister that he would not sell the box because 'I suppose it will be amongst the last of her precious gifts'.

The Pembrokeshire press followed the nationals in its jingoistic coverage of the war, highlighting the cruelty of the Boers. In one report of June 1901, the *Telegraph* contrasted the heroic pluck of two Haverfordwest brothers (William and Jim Morgan) with the cowardly actions of the Boers, which included shooting at a doctor and ambulance, attacking horses and abusing the privilege of the white flag.

Despite the censorship of letters home, occasional references to British mistakes slipped through. In 1899, Grenadier William Acraman wrote to his mother in Fishguard about the failure to shell a position in Griqualand before they stormed it – 'our poor boys fell fast in a terrible cross-fire'.

The 'war fever' featured in the 'Khaki' election campaign of October 1900 with war critics, notably David Lloyd George, denounced as traitors. John Philipps, Liberal MP for Pembroke, was also critical of the Conservative Government's handling of the war, including the accusation of 'horse murder' by sending cheap and unwieldy animals selected from around the world, many of whom were unsuited for the sparse veldt of South Africa.

The horses, arriving incapacitated and dehydrated, were sent to the front with no time to acclimatise. Bombardier Fred Pearce of the Royal Horse Artillery recalled seeing the land strewn with dead horses and mules, while several parties were deployed to shoot horses that were no longer capable of working. He observed hundreds dying from hunger and overwork. He taught his own horse to drink from a water bottle while he was lost on the veldt. However, it became so thin that he had to cover it with a tarpaulin to stop the sun setting fire to the little amount of grass in its stomach.

In total, the war claimed the lives of more than 300,000 horses. One of Peace's duties was to bury them, and on one such occasion, he caught enteric fever (typhoid) under the broiling heat, which eventually led to his passage home to Haverfordwest.

The editor of *The Haverfordwest and Milford Telegraph* considered that the South African War contributed to Queen Victoria's declining health. She did not live to see the end of the war, when peace terms were signed in 1902 which recognised British military administration over Transvaal and the Orange Free State while granting an amnesty to the Boer forces.

In 1904, a memorial was erected in Haverfordwest to remember forty-four of the Pembrokeshire men who died in the war. The British scorched-earth policy of burning Boer farms and the use of new concentration camps attracted growing public criticism and was to seriously damage the Empire's reputation. The economic impact was also felt – no British war since 1815 had proven so costly (estimated at £200 million), which only quickened Britain's economic decline.

The second issue that continued to dominate the Edwardian press was closer to home. It was the long-running campaign by Nonconformists and secularists who opposed paying tithes to the Church of England in Wales. Bills for disestablishment were presented to Parliament in 1886, 1892, 1894, 1909 and 1912, but all were defeated by the House of Lords. While the Bishop of St Davids conceded that the majority of Welsh people wanted disestablishment, he warned about the dangers of secularisation, 'the growth of materialism and indifference', which posed great harm, especially in the towns and industrial districts of South Wales.

In 1909, the Rector of Tenby argued that to break up the sacred Church and State alliance, formed over many centuries, would imperil the status of religion in national life. However, such arguments had little political traction and by 1914 the Welsh Church Act created an independent but non-established Church of Wales, to take effect in 1920.

Religion mattered to many people in the 1900s, as the famous Welsh Revival of 1904–5 illustrated. James Williams remembered in his Edwardian childhood an old man who walked in his clogs from Fishguard to Cilgerran, some 20 miles, to attend the Sunday services at 10 a.m., 2 p.m. and 6 p.m. and would then discuss the sermons with fellow travellers as he returned on foot in the evening.

Williams himself was impressed by the sermons of Jubilee Young, born in Maencholog, who became president of the Welsh Baptist Union. In our more secular age of Sunday shopping and sport, it is difficult to imagine packed congregations, including many youngsters, hanging on the preacher's every word. The likes of Young were princes of the pulpit, great showmen and highly skilled orators who created moments of sheer ecstasy:

> The veins of his neck and temples stood out, while streamlets of sweat made furrows down his face. His collar and tie became sodden, proof that he was wrestling mightily on their behalf. He was on a 'hot' line to God.

The third matter of national interest was the campaign to extend the vote to women. Interestingly, Queen Victoria herself was famously against women's suffrage. At the start of her reign, political power in Pembrokeshire rested in the hands of Conservative landowners, such as the Cawdors and Campbells.

However, the national ascendancy of the Liberal Party was such that in the General Election of 1900, the Liberals won twenty-eight out of thirty-four Welsh seats, narrowly losing out by just twelve votes to the Conservatives in Pembroke and Haverfordwest (although this was overturned in subsequent elections). Historically, the Liberal Party was sympathetic to franchise reform and women's rights. However, when Prime Minister Henry Campbell Bannerman was replaced by anti-suffragist Herbert Asquith in 1908, the government's position changed. As the actress and suffragette Elizabeth Robins put it, 'The women's cause lost a weak friend and gained a determined enemy.'

Not all women supported the vote. In 1909, the *Tenby Observer* carried an article titled 'Feminine Rule Without the Vote' to describe the women of Llangwm. It reported that the village was 'essentially a woman's colony' where women made all the financial decisions, including what clothes the men should wear on Sundays. Many worked as fisherwomen travelling two or three times a week by ferryboat or foot to Pembroke or Haverfordwest to dispose of their catches of oysters. The most famous was Dorothy 'Dolly' Palmer, who inspired paintings, postcards and newspaper articles. She died at the age of 90 in 1932, having carried paniers of oysters on her back two or three times a week over 70 years. The husbands stayed at home carrying out domestic duties. While they were staunch Liberal supporters, they despised the vote 'as something for degenerative women in the big towns and cities, but as altogether unnecessary to those who possess their Spartan heroism'.

The Llangwm women were not impressed by Emmeline Pankhurst, Annie Kenney and other leading suffragettes who visited the county in 1908 on their 'Votes for Women' campaign. Pankhurst and her fellow campaigners arrived to oppose the Liberal candidate Walter Roch, even though he was personally a supporter of women's suffrage. Their stance was based on Roch's position as Asquith's man.

More than 1,000 people listened to Pankhurst at a speech she delivered in Castle Square, Haverfordwest. At Fishguard's Market Square, the newspapers reported that the largest ever open-air meeting was held in the town's history when Rosamund Massey and Nellie Martel addressed the crowd from a wagonette. The audience did not appreciate the attack on Lloyd George, whose father was born in Pembrokeshire. Hecklers interrupted the speeches with laughter and threw pepper on the ground to make people sneeze to add further interruption.

In general, however, the suffragettes were respectfully listened to as they travelled around the county. They showed remarkable resolution and endurance, despite imprisonment and physical assaults. Their cause gained further support when the campaign was suspended during the First World War and women contributed significantly to the war effort, notably working in munitions factories.

A SENSIBLE WHEELING COSTUME.

Two Cycling Suits.

Fig. 20 Pembrokeshire bicycle advertisements from the 1890s, many of which were aimed at women.

But perhaps the most important contribution to women's liberation was the development of the humble bicycle (Figure 20). Freewheeling to equality, women could escape the watchful gaze of chaperones and the drudgery of domestic life, even if only for a few hours.

George Ace, a former amateur Welsh cycling champion, opened a cycle shop in Tenby in 1884 and soon cashed in on the cycle craze. Tenby Cycling Club is still called the Tenby Aces.

Cycling was something that 'wheeled women' of all classes enjoyed. In 1896, a rather bemused Princess Maud, Queen Victoria's granddaughter, received forty-eight bicycles as wedding gifts. One potential sticking point was what to wear, with much debate over whether the donning of loose cycling breeches conveyed a semi-masculine appearance.

Cycling became a major means of transport for many rural workers. In the 1950s, my own grandfather cycled each day from Newport to Haverfordwest, a near-40-mile round trip, to work on a farm.

Cycling in the countryside, seaside picnics and garden parties are among the enduring images of the Edwardian era portrayed as the 'good old days' when the sun never set on the British Empire. Initially, there were signs of optimism in the Liberal Government's programme of social reforms, which offered, for example, pensions for the over 70s, free school meals, health insurance for low-paid workers and labour exchanges to help unemployed people find work. As it turned out, the reforms were soon overshadowed by economic constraints and other international priorities.

11

THE FIRST WORLD WAR

The First World War is associated with images of trench warfare, mud, blood, gas and no man's land. Other aspects of the war, however, have also been increasingly portrayed, reflecting a shift away from depicting military operations towards the wider human experience, for example, in civilian life on the home front and how the war has been remembered. In Pembrokeshire, the *Western Telegraph* published 'The Great War' (2014), an eight-page supplement which highlighted the contribution made by people from the county and how the war's centenary was to be commemorated. The human dimension is also well covered in *Pembroke Remembers* (2019), produced by the Pembroke & Monkton Local History Society. The last of the First World War veterans may have died in 2009, but interest in the conflict shows no sign of receding.

THE OUTBREAK OF WAR

On 1 July 1914, readers of the local and national *Telegraph* woke up to the news that Archduke Franz Ferdinand of Austria and his wife Sophie had been assassinated during their visit to the Bosnian capital, Sarajevo, a few days earlier. Almost the same amount of column inches were given to the death of Richard Davies, a Pembrokeshire man working in a Tredegar pit. Such news was likely to have been of more interest to locals than far-off events in Bosnia. However, their lives were to be transformed by the First World War in unimaginable ways.

Britain declared war on Germany on 4 August 1914. In the evening, sober-minded Neyland county councillors debated whether to defer the employment of a lamplighter to save money because it feared that the town would feel 'the pinch of war'. On more pressing matters, it anticipated that 2,000 troops were to be stationed at Scoveston Fort alone. This clearly sharpened their thinking, and the appointment was approved because, as one councillor explained, 'it would be dangerous to life with motor cars flying through the town to remain in darkness'.

In Pembrokeshire, the response to the war was led by Colonel Ivor Philipps of Cosheston Hall, who was chairman of the county council. He was a military man, having served with distinction in both China and India before beginning a new career in the petroleum business.

During the Battle of the Somme, General Haig dismissed Philipps from his command of the 38th Division because he lacked 'push', although Philipps had been constricted by the orders sent from headquarters. Despite slurs against his character, including resentment over his political connections, Philipps was knighted for his services during the war.

Pembrokeshire's military connections contributed to a general mood of excitement and support for the war. *The Haverfordwest and Milford Telegraph* reported on 5 August that feelings of loyalty and patriotism were evident through the county as war fever had spread across Europe.

Only twenty or so conscientious objectors took a stance against the war in Pembrokeshire, citing religious, moral or political arguments. They faced tribunal hearings to explain what they would do if the Germans attacked, for example, their mother or sister. In 1916, 19-year-old Thomas Thomas informed the Fishguard tribunal that wearing khaki was a sign of the Antichrist and he would save neither his mother nor his sister if he was obliged to do so.

The court of public opinion had little time for perceived cowards and shirkers, and yet the liberty of conscience was a deeply ingrained British tradition. Most rural tribunals, which were not dominated by military men, had some sympathy for applicants who worked in such industries as farming but were far less inclined to grant exemptions for those who objected to fight on conscientious grounds. The congregationalist minister, T.E. Nicholas ('Niclas y Glais'), who was brought up in Pembrokeshire, was an anti-war poet whose sermons were monitored by the authorities, who feared his Marxist leanings and potential treasonable sentiments.

But such voices formed a small minority. The *Telegraph* reassured its readers that Pembrokeshire was well prepared for 'a hostile invasion', with six trains laden with troops arriving every night. Much of south Pembrokeshire, especially around Milford Haven, became a militarised zone. A series of sea and land forts, trenches, hutted camps and tents dotted the landscape. Penally Camp, which has a military history dating back to 1860 as a musketry camp, was the most significant and continues to function as a training centre. During the First World War, Penally Camp comprised officers' and soldiers' quarters, a sergeants' mess, an ablutions block, hospital, cookhouse, canteen, magazine, guardhouse, storerooms and two underground water tanks. There were also offsite trench systems on the clifftops and at Yeomanry Field, alongside rifle ranges and training grounds, key aspects of preparing soldiers for war.

Three airfields were established at the Marine Operations (Balloon) Station at Milford Haven, the Flying Boat Base at Fishguard and the Airship Station between Carew and Sageston (RNAS Pembroke), all concerned with submarine patrols and escorting convoys. For locals, particularly schoolchildren, these were exciting times, with the arrival of thousands of soldiers and the sights and sounds of despatch riders, horses, battalion cyclists, billeted men around the towns, parades, the construction of huts and tented campsites.

The threat of a German invasion was taken seriously because of Milford Haven's strategic value as a deep-water port. Although none of the forts came under attack, their presence, along with fire trenches, searchlights, gun emplacements and extensive wire entanglements, acted as a deterrent.

Dale Fort was used as a signal station, while Chapel Bay Fort (at Angle) became an 'Examination Battery', manned twenty-four hours a day and monitoring shipping entering and leaving the estuary. Ships suspected of running munitions or food to Germany were detained and the captains directed not to leave the waterway, or they would be fired upon. In recent years, the site has been restored and turned into Chapel Bay Fort and Museum.

The first German prisoner was captured in September 1914 when a search of a steamer, which had pulled into Milford Haven for coals, found a 27-year-old German among the crew. He had an English wife but in a time of heightened tensions was handed over to the military. He was probably detained at either Drim Wood, Narberth or another camp at Haverfordwest. Around 20,000 out of 70,000 German subjects living in the UK were interned during the war.

The immediate impact of the war saw an increase in food prices. Shopkeepers in Haverfordwest reported abuse from customers within days of war being declared. By June 1915, food prices rose by 32 per cent and increased by a similar amount in the following year. In January 1917, the German policy of unrestricted submarine warfare further reduced British supplies and put added strain on the supply chain. Local ration schemes were introduced from December 1917, beginning with sugar and subsequently extended to other foodstuffs, including jam, butter, bacon and margarine.

Adults were issued with ration books containing detachable coupons. Local food committees were responsible for administration, including the setting of maximum prices. These committees varied in their efficiency, with consumers complaining about a lack of transparency, high prices and long queues.

Breaches of food regulations included grocers who did not display prices, fruit sold outside approved dates and bacon obtained without coupons. Despite the pressures on food supply and rising prices, an official enquiry into the working-class cost of living conducted after the war found that families of unskilled workmen were slightly better fed in 1918 than they were in 1914. Historians have since reappraised this and conclude that while the calorie intakes were on average maintained for low-wage households, more prosperous families experienced a fall in their fat intake.

WAR STORIES

Almost immediately after the war began, the Pembrokeshire press publicised reports of German atrocities which set the tone of the wartime narrative. The *Telegraph* relayed to its readers how Germans had burnt churches with worshippers, including women and children, inside or had shot whole streets of people as they invaded Belgium. Some of these stories were well founded, although the majority of victims were men of military age who were suspected of being snipers.

Inhumane acts on non-combatants were committed by both sides. Early in the war, a local newspaper reporter interviewed one Belgian refugee in Milford Haven, who claimed 'the Germans had entered her friends' homes in Belgium and killed babies and even cats and birds'. Four years later, the Merchant Seamen's League who met at Milford were in no doubt over the 'devilish work perpetrated by the Hun'. In retaliation, the members agreed that they would not employ German workers in any capacity, they would refuse to buy or use any German goods or services and all master mariners would boycott saluting the German flag for a period of two years after hostilities ceased.

Private James Vaughan of Haverfordwest survived the Battle of Ypres. While he had not personally seen German cruelty, his fellow soldiers told him that they had seen more than one child 'whose arm or hand had been cut off by the enemy'. Vaughan also explained that he had seen piles of up to fifty German bodies buried in large graves. It is easy to forget that each of these had a family at home. Vaughan claimed he witnessed marauding half-drunken German soldiers and German artillery attacks which resulted in coffins at the Festubert Cemetery being exposed.

In May 1918, writing from Palestine, Private Fred Williams from Haverfordwest summed up his trench experience, 'where the living die and the dying live'.

Pembrokeshire men were among the very first wartime casualties. On 6 August, just thirty-six hours into the war, HMS *Amphion*, which was built in Pembroke Dock in 1911, became the first Royal Navy ship to be sunk. It hit a mine in the North Sea after successfully sinking a German mine-laying ship. Although the crew were initially rescued by escorting destroyers, as the frigate drifted it hit further mines and the exploding debris struck the rescue boats and destroyers. Among the fatalities was Albert Martin ('Stoker'), a 26-year-old from Milford Haven.

The first Pembrokeshire man killed on land was possibly Stuart Kirby Jones, the council's veterinary inspector. Aged 25, he was shipped to France on 14 August, where he was appointed Veterinary Officer in charge of the 25th Brigade, Royal Field Artillery and posted to the Western Front. During the First Battle of the Aisne, Lieutenant Jones found himself on the Moulins to

Bourg Road and turned his horse to the side to take a moment to read a letter from home. Moments later, a large German shell landed a few yards away and his leg was shattered by a fragment. Although he was patched up by a field ambulance and sent to a hospital near Versailles, he deteriorated and died on 18 September 1914. He is buried in Versailles. The chaplain sent his mother a piece of heather he took from the cemetery a few yards from her son's grave. It is these individual stories that show how the war touched the lives of Pembrokeshire families.

PASSENGERS CLINGING TO A SOMERSAULTING LIFEBOAT OF THE BRITISH AFRICAN LINER FALABA, TORPE-DOED AND SUNK BY A GERMAN SUBMARINE
(Photos © by International News Service.)

Fig. 21 Passengers rescued from the *Falaba*. (The New York Times, *18 April 1915, https://www.loc.gov*)

Offshore, the German U-boats were a major threat to British shipping. On 28 March 1915, RMS *Falaba* (Figure 21), which left Liverpool bound for Sierra Leone, was torpedoed off the Pembrokeshire coast with the loss of 104 lives. Her wreck lies some 38 miles to the west of the Smalls Reef. At the sinking of the *Falaba*, one eyewitness vividly described the scene:

> I saw seven men upon the deck of the German submarine laughing and jeering at the struggle of our people. After our vessel sank, and when these who had been sucked down by her came to the surface they held up their hands, making frantic efforts to grab at anything. This seemed to cause intense amusement amongst the pirates on the submarine, who laughed at and ridiculed the frantic efforts of our poor fellows, and then, after circling round the scene and making sure their dastardly work was only too well done, partially submerged their raft, and made off without offering assistance or caring whether there was any near at hand.

Another observed:

> I had to cling to a line and let myself down into the boat with
> shrapnel flying around me, and the boatswain, who was by my
> side, received awful wounds and fell back on deck. I could see it
> was no use trying to do anything for him.

Many First World War survivors were unwilling to talk about
their experiences, whether during leave, immediately after the war
or later in life. Private James Vaughan was among the few who
did. He spoke about his near-death experiences, including seeing
a German shell land 20 yards away, killing a group of six men
instantly. On another occasion, he heard the rush of air as a shell
passed close to his head, blowing his cap clean off. Vaughan also
described when he was on sentry duty his nervous reaction upon
hearing the crackling of twigs. Stooping, he detected a silhouetted
figure against the dark skyline. He shouted a challenge and, following no response, opened fire. He had shot what was concluded
to be a German spy dressed in civilian clothes. The German had
been carrying a bible, which Vaughan kept as a souvenir.

This account appeared in a letter which was published by the
Telegraph. All such letters were partial descriptions – as Trooper
W.T. Lewis put it, 'I could describe many events, but they would
not pass the censor'. Nonetheless, such correspondence offers
insight into wartime conditions – the mud, prolonged periods of
silence, the camaraderie, maiming and death of friends and coun-
trymen, seen one moment and gone the next. They also reveal the
values of the age.

Lewis, from Haverfordwest, served with the Indian
Expeditionary Force on 'police work', stationed in an Indian camp
by a large lake in the Artois region of France. He had 'two native
servants who do all the cooking and the food is very good'. The
censors had no trouble in allowing veiled criticisms of the Indian
soldiers. Lewis admitted that they were 'very fine fellows', but
soon kicked up a fuss when it was their turn to go out on patrol
'beating tom-toms and performed war dances'.

The Indian Expeditionary Force had been sent to France and
Belgium in September 1914 and held part of the front line against
the German Army until October 1915. It is an often overlooked

fact that nearly a third of the 8.5 million men who made up the British forces in the First World War were *not* British. India supplied 1.4 million men to the Allied war effort, more than the combined efforts of Wales, Ireland and Scotland. And while the likes of Trooper Lewis may have sneered at what he perceived to be their fight-shy tendencies, 500 Indian soldiers were killed and 1,500 wounded at the Battle of Neuve Chapelle alone. It is only in recent years that their sacrifice and bravery has attracted the deserved attention amid wider debates around colonialism and the teaching of a more representative and inclusive history in schools.

The role of the press was very much to convey uplifting stories of soldiers who endured the privations of war or exemplified British values. Jack Davies, a sailor from Haverfordwest, had a narrow escape when his boat was torpedoed. He gave a vivid account to his parents, who passed the story onto the *Telegraph*. Sparing details of 'names, dates, places, and times or anything of military importance', Davies recounted how he was doing clerical work when he was suddenly shaken off his feet. When he arrived at his post, it was clear the ship was sinking fast but 'there was no stampede, everybody knew what had happened and everybody behaved like Britishers'. Unfortunately, the rope for his raft was cut and it fell to the sea with no one on board. His only option was to jump into the sea, where he was immediately carried under water and towards the stern. He swallowed lots of salt water and was then hit on the head by a falling raft but managed to stay afloat by dodging the swell of the sea. His salvation came in the form of an oar, which he grabbed hold of and he was then picked up by a rescue boat.

The war had surreal moments. Private Fred Williams of Haverfordwest recalled crossing a valley and hearing a divisional band play 'Home Sweet Home' on a stretch of barren, sunburnt land. It is unclear whether he imagined this, but he likened the experience to an invisible angelic choir, a mystical rapture interrupted only by the whizz of enemy bullets in the blue sky and the shriek of shells drowning the melody. It was a moment when 'beauty and terror' mingled, the struggle of 'annihilation and existence'.

November 1915 was a particularly difficult month to endure, with freezing temperatures causing widespread trench foot, exacerbated by strong northerly winds. Elsewhere along the Western Front, Pembrokeshire men reported shouted conversations across the British and German trenches, comparing the depth of the ice-cold water. 'Up to our blooming knees', in the case of one English corporal, and 'We're up to our belts in it,' replied a German soldier.

William Cousins of Haverfordwest recalled 'strange conversations' he held with the enemy in their trenches, which suggests how close they were to each other. 'A Bavarian regiment once shouted across, "You leave us alone today and we'll leave you alone."' Both parties agreed. There were even moments when both sides suspended shooting at each other to watch air duels.

In some places, there was a considerable degree of respect between the fighting forces. Private Arthur Davies from Haverfordwest recalled his experience at the Battle of the Somme in 1916 and relayed how the Germans 'fought with the utmost bravery and tenacity, contesting every inch of the ground'. At Delville Wood, Davies observed how 'well-directed German artillery sent brave men to their doom'. He found that the German trenches were in some cases '24 feet deep and furnished with fittings, furniture and pictures that were real works of art'.

Most accounts of the war focus on fallen combatants and the major battle sites, which has tended to overshadow the civilian casualties, including the millions of refugees scattered around Europe. Following the German invasion of Belgium, Saundersfoot was among the towns which set up a Belgian Refugees Committee.

Around 4,500 Belgian refugees were hosted in Wales. Milford alone accepted 1,000, building on long-standing ties between Pembrokeshire and the Flemish fishing communities. In 1914, twenty-four fishing boats and two steam trawlers left Ostend for Milford carrying refugees who included staff and pupils from the Belgian Royal School. The Belgians remained until September 1919. The Belgian boat owners erected a monument in Hamilton Terrace to express their gratitude.

Belgians were not the only refugees. Serbians arrived in Letterston in 1918 to help with the summer harvest, camping on the Common, while Russian Jews formed part of a Labour Corps restoring a military camp at Dale.

WAR AND NATURE

Often overlooked in the historiography of the First World War is how soldiers interacted with nature. This is significant, given that many of the Pembrokeshire army recruits were men who had worked with animals, for example as agricultural labourers or farmers.

From an environmental perspective, battlegrounds were similar to polluted industrial wastelands. Shells on the front damaged the land, just as factories did at home. Caught up in the carnage were huge numbers of mules, horses, dogs, pigeons and camels, among other creatures.

Rats tormented troops during the day and at night. Colonel Hugh Higgon, from Manorbier, used a team of sixteen ferrets to hunt the thousands of rats at Ypres. One of the Australian soldiers preferred an axe.

When war was declared in August, War Office representatives visited Haverfordwest for the purpose of buying horses but made it clear that it only wanted 'quiet ones', subject to their veterinary examination. Given the abundant supply of horses nationally, they were confident of finding suitable animals. The mass slaughter of horses at the front, captured so vividly in Steven Spielberg's film *War Horse* (2011), eroded such confidence. In 1917, the Board of Agriculture reported the desperate shortage of farm horses, which inhibited the production of food and forced the army to agree to the temporary loan of mules and draught horses to any farms near their bases in England and Wales.

In September 1919, an editorial in the *Telegraph* asked, 'What of the animals?' as it reflected on their 'splendid services', not only in conveying ammunition, messages and food through waterlogged roads where machines could not travel, but also in bringing comfort to men's suffering in the frozen trenches. Dogs acted as confidants, as well as pillows and foot-warmers. The newspaper applauded the action of the Royal Society for the Prevention of Cruelty to Animals (RSPCA) in bringing home 500 soldiers' dogs.

The RSPCA was among those who campaigned for medicines to support the Army Veterinary Corps in caring for sick and wounded horses, with donations from Welsh branches, and to tighten regulations on the safe transport home of old army horses.

Private James Vaughan of Haverfordwest thought that the horses at the front did not take much notice of the deafening noises. He was mistaken. Horses suffered trauma and serious physical suffering from gas, skin disorders and starvation.

However, it was birdsong that gave Vaughan the most comfort. During the lull between the firing, he would frequently hear the cuckoo, 'while the mellow notes of a blackbird would come floating over the trenches'.

HONOURING SOLDIERS AND SAILORS

The Pembrokeshire authorities took opportunities to honour the bravery of its soldiers, which also helped to maintain morale at home. In 1917, the Milford town crier was sent around to ask townspeople to decorate their houses to welcome home 21-year-old Private Hubert William Lewis, who had been awarded the Victoria Cross. He was greeted at the railway station by a band playing 'See the Conquering Hero Comes'. The trawlers in the docks where he formerly worked as a fish packer welcomed him with sirens. He was driven back to Hamilton Terrace, where he was carried on shoulders to his parents' home.

Lewis was the youngest Welsh recipient of the VC, the highest military decoration for conspicuous bravery and devotion to duty. His particular actions in October 1916 involved searching enemy dugouts, where he was three times wounded and at one point faced three German soldiers, whom he captured on his own. Lewis also went to the assistance of a wounded man and under heavy rifle fire carried him back to the British lines, collapsing from exhaustion.

Remarkably, Lewis returned to action in the Balkans and performed a similar feat in saving a captain in 1918 amid a gas attack during an assault on an enemy position. After the war, Lewis returned to work as a trader and then became foreman of an ice company for more than forty years. He was the last surviving Welsh Victoria Cross recipient from the First World War before his death in 1977. In 2016, to mark the hundredth anniversary of his bravery, a memorial was erected in the town's memorial gardens.

The erection of memorials throughout the county not only honoured those who had fallen but acted as a kind of emotional catharsis, so that families could move on with their lives as best they could. Simon Hancock estimates that around 5,000 Pembrokeshire people had experienced personal bereavement, on the accepted formula that, on average, each fatality affected six close relatives.

The county's graveyards include the remains of bodies washed ashore from ships and U-boats sunk during the war. These include Shiro Okosie, buried in Angle Graveyard on 16 October 1918. He was among 270 or so passengers who died when the ocean liner *Hirano Maru* was sunk, south of Ireland, by a German U-boat. In 2018, the Duke of Gloucester unveiled a granite obelisk memorial engraved in Japanese, English and Welsh, at a ceremony attended by dignitaries from the Japanese shipping line.

THE IMPACT OF THE WAR

The First World War undoubtedly transformed people's lives. It is no exaggeration to say that the war affected every man, woman and child to one degree or another. There were big changes, such as the rise of the trade unions, the decline of the aristocracy (many sons serving as officers were killed, creating inheritance problems), female emancipation and medical advances – doctors experimented with radical and potentially life-saving surgeries.

Poignantly, the number of widows and spinsters grew dramatically and many children lost their fathers. Even their school lessons changed. The Pembrokeshire Education Committee offered schools a list of war trophies for study, including German rifles, a set of body armour, wire cutters, water bottles, helmets and a Turkish bayonet. Children could also pay 3*d* to climb on board an ex-German submarine which was berthed at Milford Docks and then later at Pembroke Dock.

But the most obvious impact of the war was the sheer loss of life and the long-term emotional scars associated with a lost generation. In June 1919, the *Telegraph* reported that 880 soldiers and sailors from the county had been confirmed as being killed in the First World War but added that the figures were likely to rise to around 1,000.

The uncertainty reflected the difficulties in calculating exact numbers, given the political sensitivities of reporting casualties and the practical challenges of tracing those who were missing in action. Put simply, no one knows exactly how many people from Pembrokeshire died in the First World War.

On statistics alone, however, more people died from the flu pandemic in 1918 than were killed at war. The historian Russell Davies points out that Spanish Flu claimed 9,000 lives in Wales in four months (and 20,000 died in Wales during 1914–18) and yet 'there is almost no echo of a cough in the history books'. Perhaps this is because of the uniqueness of the first ever global war and the indelible stain it left on communities then and over succeeding generations.

One interpretation of the war's impact suggests that it shook the foundations of religious certainty and ushered in a whole new world, from people's diets and work patterns to entertainment and the availability of goods and services. Others contest that the change was more gradual and began in the Edwardian pre-war years, while some commentators suggest that the war actually reinforced conservatism and a desire to return to the perceived former days of imperial glory.

It was soon clear to observers when the war ended that the world would never be the same. There was much talk of reconstruction, but as the editor of the *Telegraph* predicted a week before the armistice agreement, 'We shall be wise to recognise that Peace will be followed by change and upheaval; by considerable unemployment, and, possibly, by unfortunate sex antagonisms'.

On the last point, he was alluding to the tensions created as servicemen returned to a shortage of jobs and a society in which women's roles had changed, traditional boundaries had been blurred and political freedoms extended. In 1918, the Representation of the People Act granted the vote to women over the age of 30 who met a property qualification. Nonetheless, this fell far short of suffragette calls for electoral equality. The mass dismissal of women who had worked in factories during the war to make way for men returning from the front may have satisfied the male trade unions but it was a reminder that women still had a long way to go before they achieved equality.

12

THE INTERWAR YEARS

The interwar years are renowned for mass unemployment, the great banking crisis and the Depression. This period saw the last throws of the British Empire and the seeds of an increasingly secular, consumer society. Initially, there was understandably huge public relief at the end of the Great War, but the marks of that war did not end in 1918. A report by the Pembrokeshire Education Committee issued in 1921 summed up the change of mood between 'the immediate post-war period of burning enthusiasm and ardent desire to sacrifice for the nation's ultimate good and the present period of stringent and sometimes unreasoning economy'.

Those returning to Pembrokeshire from the services bore their wounds, both psychological and physical. Physically wounded returning soldiers hobbled around the Pembrokeshire towns and villages. Many carried psychological scars for the rest of their lives. Organisations such as the Comrades of the Great War and the North Pembrokeshire Association of Discharged and Demobilised Sailors and Soldiers did what they could to help rehabilitate and represent the rights of ex-servicemen and women. The war may have ended but the interwar years proved exceptionally difficult times for the average Pembrokeshire family.

Adjusting to peacetime was not straightforward for many returning servicemen. Finding appropriate work was a major challenge, particularly for older men and those with disabilities or psychological problems. In 1918, the Ministry of Pensions published a *Disabled Soldiers' Handbook*, which set out arrangements for state pensions and compensation for injuries. The two emboldened messages were 'get as well and keep as well as you can' and 'get back to work of a kind that you can stick to'. Such

well-intentioned but patronising tones failed to grasp the significance of the practical, psychological and emotional barriers that
many demobilised men faced.

At the most basic of levels, in December 1918, the
Haverfordwest postmaster led a local appeal for the donations
of sturdy walking sticks for wounded soldiers, to meet a national
shortage. At a deeper level, over the course of the war, around
80,000 British soldiers were treated for 'wounded minds'. After
1917, psychiatrists dubbed this 'shell shock'.

The government acknowledged that it was important to
exclude servicemen who had fought to save civilisation from the
stigma of certification for insanity and being detained alongside
paupers in lunatic asylums. Instead, efforts were made to utilise
civilian hospitals, but the growing number of casualties meant
that the authorities eventually had to rely on regular asylums. A
steady stream of Pembrokeshire men were sent to the Carmarthen
Asylum, albeit under a new category of 'Service Patients', which
brought the benefits of additional comforts and an allowance.

In seeking to form a reconstructed society, Lloyd George's post-
war government conceived a range of reforms, notably in health,
housing and education. Unfortunately, such plans were curtailed
or abandoned following the 1921 worldwide economic slump.
The agricultural and industrial production stimulated by the
war effort declined sharply. Locally, the closure of the Pembroke
Dockyard in 1926 was a major blow.

By 1937, more than one in two of the insured population in
Pembrokeshire was unemployed. Thousands left the county in
search for employment in new industries, such as vehicle manufac-
turing and electrical engineering in the Midlands and south-east of
England. Farmers, who had seen higher prices in the war, suffered as
proceeds from sheep, cattle and crop sales collapsed. Although the
government had introduced the Agricultural Act of 1920 to stabilise
the market by offering a four-year guarantee of prices for selected
farm produce, it was forced to repeal this within a year because of
the national debt and a world surplus of food. This became known
as the 'Great Betrayal' and angered British farmers.

The population drift from the countryside left farms increasingly vulnerable and many farm buildings fell into disrepair. The
long decline in agriculture persisted through to the Second World

War, although farmers received a boost in the 1930s when the newly created Milk Marketing Board introduced the Milk in School scheme, which created a new market.

Children's welfare and education was central to the post-war reconstruction plans. For example, the Maternity and Child Welfare Act 1918 established infant welfare clinics at Goodwick, Fishguard, Newport, Milford Haven, Pembroke Dock, Solva, Narberth and Haverfordwest. From these, free milk was distributed to 'necessitous' mothers and children under school age, as well as nursing mothers.

As the county Medical Health Officer pointed out, expenditure was heavy because of the intense poverty throughout Pembrokeshire caused by unemployment. District nurses and health visitors provided home visits and, more generally, medical advances contributed to the eradication of diseases and a gradual decline in both maternal and infant mortality rates.

There were certain endemic diseases, such as the disfiguring and highly contagious smallpox, which was not eradicated until the 1970s. Whooping cough was another persistent health threat that forced the periodic closure of schools. In 1922 alone, nine children died in the county from whooping cough. Tuberculosis was also a major concern. The Welsh National Memorial Association managed the county's two dedicated hospitals – at Sealyham (near Wolfscastle) for adults and at St Bride's for children. St Bride's employed two surgeons, twenty-three nurses and three resident teachers. Children requiring specialist, prolonged orthopaedic treatment were sent to Cardiff, Oswestry or London.

THE 'ROARING TWENTIES'

It would be misleading to think that the interwar years were a period of unrelenting gloom. On the contrary, sales of telephones increased, vacuum cleaners and other technologies made household chores so much easier, and more and more people flocked to the cinemas in Haverfordwest, Tenby, Pembroke, Narberth, Neyland, Fishguard and Milford Haven.

For the wealthy, automobiles were much sought after. Green's Motors of Haverfordwest sold its first motor car in 1907. The Pembrokeshire Automobile Club was very active, arranging regular 'runs' around the county. Naturally, its members were drawn from the well-to-do in society, such as Colonel Phillips and Ralph Green. Reminiscent of a scene from *Downtown Abbey*, on a beautiful summer's day in July 1910, a party of a dozen or so motorists sped out on the country lanes to the magnificent grounds of the Ffynone Estate (at Boncath), where they delighted in tennis and croquet, quenched their thirst with nectarines and arrived back in Haverfordwest at eight o'clock in the evening. The wealthy knew how to enjoy themselves – one of their amusements was for each driver, accompanied by a lady, to drop a potato into a bucket as the car went by. Spiffing.

Moving pictures had been shown before the First World War, for example, through such pioneering showmen as William Haggar and his Royal Electric Bioscope, who visited Portfield Fair, in Haverfordwest, and Pembroke Fair. Haggar went on to establish indoor cinemas throughout South Wales, including the one that bore his name in Pembroke.

The county's most impressive cinema was Shanly's in Tenby's South Beach Pavilion, which opened in 1929. This six-storey entertainment centre included a 660-seat cinema, dance hall, amusement arcades, roof gardens, skating rink, confectionary booths and shops. It finally closed in 1975 and was demolished soon after. These cinemas enabled people to enjoy, for an hour or two, a make-believe world far removed from their daily struggles.

Pembrokeshire was a long way from the lights of London and other cities, but this did not mean that the 'Roaring Twenties' bypassed West Wales. New styles of clothing, dance and manners penetrated even the remotest corners.

The decade was symbolised by Flappers, originally a term for prostitutes, who were highly spirited young women determined to enjoy life. They smoked cigarettes, danced to jazz, the new music of the decade, attended outlandish parties, drank alcohol and generally challenged the norms associated with femininity. They were very different in appearance and manner to the utilitarian Land Girls who had conscientiously worked on the Pembrokeshire farms from 1917. As Simon Hancock says, the latter were 'dressed in outfits more reminiscent of the Wild West'.

In their pursuit of joy, the Flappers pushed the boundaries of modesty, beginning with lowering their hemlines. The more conservative confined themselves to actions such as catching a ride on a soldier's bicycle at Neyland to show off an ankle or two. The more risqué wore tight-fitting bathing costumes on Tenby beach and enjoyed the pleasures of mixed bathing.

Such gaiety drowned the sorrows of the war and brought temporary relief from the misery of unemployment, the chief problem of the age, and its associated social, emotional and psychological consequences. The Great Depression of the 1930s witnessed increased rates of suicide for all age groups in England and Wales.

While the social and economic strain was most widely reported in the coal-mining valleys of South Wales, Pembrokeshire communities also suffered, particularly in the shipbuilding yards around Milford Haven and Pembroke Dock. It was hard to find reasons to be cheerful when the optimism of building 'a country fit for heroes' quickly evaporated. Those words were uttered by David Lloyd George in 1918, just days after the end of the First World War. He told his audience in Wolverhampton, 'Don't let us waste this victory merely in ringing joybells.'

13

THE SECOND WORLD WAR

At the outbreak of the Second World War, it was widely feared that the civilian population would be affected far more than they had been in the First World War. Technical advances in Germany's military aircraft meant that bombers could reach Britain quickly and with lethal consequences, including the use of poison gas.

EVACUEES

Plans for protecting the most vulnerable citizens revolved around evacuating them from the large cities such as London, Liverpool and Birmingham into the countryside. Remarkably, such plans were conceived as early as 1931 and gathered pace in the 1930s as the might of the German air force developed.

An ambitious evacuation programme was finalised in 1938, somewhat disturbingly code-named Operation Pied Piper, ironically after the German folktale. It was to prove the largest social experiment of the twentieth century. From today's viewpoint, it is unsettling to think that such a mass evacuation occurred with children not told where they were going, who they might live with or when they might return home. But these were extraordinary times.

Rural Pembrokeshire was regarded as a relatively safe place for evacuees. Children were also evacuated from Pembroke Dock on a nightly basis to the village of Cosheston. The nearby Carew Cheriton Control Tower hosts a reconstructed Stanton air raid shelter, displays and memorabilia, and visitors can learn about the wartime experiences. It is located on an airfield used by the Royal Air Force during the war.

The Imperial War Museum estimates that over three days (1–3 September 1939), around 1.5 million people were evacuated as part of the official national scheme. In June 1940, around 3,200 child evacuees arrived in Pembrokeshire from the south and south-west of England. Around a third were accommodated in Haverfordwest, another third at St Dogmaels and the remainder at Fishguard and Narberth.

The threat of Hitler's V-1 flying bombs and V-2 missiles in 1944 led to a further wave of evacuation. In total, around 3 million people were evacuated during the war, with perhaps as many as 200,000 sent to Wales.

Practical challenges included transporting the evacuees, finding suitable accommodation and arranging their continued education. Disruptions were inevitable, given the voluntary basis of the evacuation, with some children staying for most of the war and forging lifelong friendships, while others returned, homesick, after a few weeks or even days. However, the surviving education records generally suggest that the transition was smooth, given the uncertainties many schools faced, from Wiston to Nevern, and from Stepaside to Fishguard. Children were taught by their teachers in church buildings and village halls when they could not be accommodated in schools.

The Ministry of Information produced upbeat photographs and films showing city children enjoying the fresh air and nature of West Wales. For example, one image shows older children from London's Deptford Park School keenly sawing logs on the estate where they were billeted in Haverfordwest. A scrapbook kept by Miss K. Wheeler, the headmistress of Hythe Senior Girls School (available on the Imperial War Museum website) includes newspaper snippets and photographs which illustrate how her students gained a range of novel learning experiences, from milking cows to participating in the North Pembrokeshire and South Cardiganshire Methodist Festival. While Welsh speakers expressed concern that the arrival of evacuees would dilute Welsh language and culture, such cultural exchanges suggested otherwise.

Despite the hospitality of the vast majority of Pembrokeshire householders, serious questions have been raised about the treatment of children who were either not welcomed or were abused in one form or another. Jewish, Irish, Roman Catholic and black children were more vulnerable and likely to encounter religious, racial or social prejudices. There were also language barriers. Maurice Levitt, a 7-year-old Jewish boy from East Hackney who was evacuated to Fishguard with his mother, recalled his experience of entering a shop in the town:

> When they saw us come us in, they started speaking Welsh. So the mothers couldn't understand what they were talking about and could be talking about them. So the Jewish mothers started talking between themselves in Yiddish.

For their part, some Pembrokeshire hosts complained about the many dirty, lice-ridden, foul-mouthed and badly behaved urban children.

GERMAN RAIDS

Even though rural Pembrokeshire was considered a safe zone, the Germans targeted towns such as Pembroke Dock for their strategic importance. The authorities tried to deceive German night-raiders into bombing open fields around Cosheston Point, rather than the naval dockyards, given the rough similarity in their shorelines. Incendiary devices were set alight to resemble burning houses and lured some bombers, resulting in reports of several cows falling victim and craters still visible in the fields.

Nonetheless, on 19 August 1940 the dockyard was set ablaze when three German Junkers escorted by fighters bombed the oil tanks at Llanreath, destroying eleven out of eighteen. The subsequent fire lasted eighteen days and is said to have been the largest in Britain since the Great Fire of London in 1666, with the palls of black smoke visible from Swansea and north Wales. It took 650 firefighters from across the UK to put the fire out, which caused more than 1,100 injuries and five fatalities among the Cardiff brigade. South Pembrokeshire Golf Club, which now occupies part of the site where the oil tanks stood, has a plaque in memory of the firemen, while Arthur Morris Drive is named after the chief fire officer who directed operations.

The attack destroyed an estimated 33 million gallons of oil. In *Pembrokeshire Under Fire*, Bill Richards describes how one family living in the western part of Bush Street suffered. Dr Harvey was seriously injured as debris from the fire landed on his home, and his wife died. Their child escaped:

> ... due to the presence of mind of Mrs Harvey who, although partly buried by the debris, and on the point of collapse, threw the child clear of the fire into the passage. There it was found uninjured hanging by its clothing on a clothes peg on the wall.

Richards was a young news reporter at the time. He recalled:

> Down the hill from Pembroke Dock they came in an endless stream, in cars, lorries and overloaded buses, on motorcycles, bicycles and horse drawn carts. Hundreds came on foot, weary mothers with infants in arms and little boys and girls of hardly school age running behind ... old men on sticks ... subdued boys and frightened girls. Nearly every person clutched tightly some valued possession ... Dogs, cats, caged birds accompanied their owners.

A further German raid on 12 May 1941 resulted in thirty-two deaths and the destruction or damage of over 2,000 homes. The last major air raid took place on Pembroke Dock on 11 June 1941 when incendiary bombs set the town alight. Thereafter, the raids eased and finally stopped in 1943. A memorial in St John's Church lists the names of known civilian casualties.

Pembrokeshire had a role to play in the main battles of the Second World War. Between July and October 1940, the Royal Air Force engaged in aerial battles against the German air force in the iconic Battle of Britain. Three of the fourteen RAF stations in Wales were located in Pembrokeshire – at Pembroke Dock, Carew Cheriton and Manorbier. Among the pilots who died were Charles Ayling, who was shot down in his Spitfire and buried at Monkton.

In the Battle of the Atlantic, which ran effectively through the whole course of the war, Pembroke Dock was the base for

Sunderland flying boats and Milford Haven became a key assembly point for naval convoys and escorts. At one time, ninety-nine planes were moored at the dockside.

DEFENDING PEMBROKESHIRE

Around 5,000 American soldiers were stationed at Llanion Barracks, while others were accommodated elsewhere around the county. Belgian soldiers were deployed in building Tenby's defences, which included installing iron rails to obstruct landing by enemy aircraft. One legend has it that Haverfordwest hosted Rocco Marchegiano, who was later to become the world's only heavyweight boxing champion to remain undefeated (under the name Rocky Marciano). In Maenclochog it is even suggested that he got caught up in his first fistfight outside the Castle Hotel and when four military policemen arrived, he floored them all. However, alternative stories place Marchegiano at Swansea with no hard evidence that he ever ventured further west.

In May 1940 the Pembrokeshire Home Guard was formed as the last line of defence. It comprised men in reserved occupations that were essential for the war effort and others who could not be called up for military service for various reasons. Nationally, around 1.7 million men served in the so-called 'Dad's Army'. Several platoons were formed in the county before they were stood down in December 1944 as the threat of a German invasion disappeared.

Certificates of Merit were awarded to those who served. In 2020, a batch of these certificates were discovered along with a tin hat in an attic in Treffgarne, where the platoon was captained by a local agricultural contractor, W.D. Bevan. Perhaps Bevan forgot to distribute these certificates.

Although some of the Home Guard members were experienced First World War veterans, the historian Norman Longmate found that there was some truth behind the more laughable scenes depicted in the popular BBC *Dad's Army* television sitcom (1968–77). In his book *The Real Dad's Army* (1974), which drew on letters from the public, Longmate demonstrated that men did go hunting for crack German paratroopers and Nazis armed only with broom handles and golf clubs. And they did mistake sheep, cows and even a stationary hedgehog for the sneakily camouflaged enemy.

On a more serious note, the military bases in Pembrokeshire during the war years witnessed several tragedies. In December 1940 and July 1941, in separate incidents, two Polish pilots were among those killed performing 'diving' sorties. They were among more than 17,000 airmen who served in the Polish Air Force stationed in Britain. Another crash in March 1943 saw two crew members on a convoy patrol die after losing control of their aircraft, which clipped a farm building and crashed into a field.

D-DAY REHEARSALS

Between July and August 1943, the beaches at Tenby, Saundersfoot, Carmarthen Bay, Swansea and Port Talbot were chosen to rehearse possible landings in Normandy as part of the top-secret Exercise Jantzen. Locals had to carry identity cards, while telephone calls and other communications were subjected to censorship and strict curfews were imposed. During thirteen days of exercises, more than 16,000 tons of supplies were brought ashore, which represented a significant logistical exercise to oversee. However, this was well short of the target set of 23,400 tons, with specific problems associated with 'Alligator' vehicles unloading and petrol spillages. Prime Minister Winston Churchill was one of the spectators who took 'a plain Welsh tea' at the Wiseman's Bridge Inn.

Overall, an official evaluation of the exercise concluded that it failed to meet its objectives. However, there were valuable lessons gained. As the commentator to the accompanying War Office film put it, 'The value of training of drivers in manoeuvring vehicles into landing crafts became very obvious', adding at one point, rather dryly, 'this is not the correct way to signal a vehicle into a landing craft'.[4]

Churchill returned again to Pembrokeshire on 1 April 1944, accompanied by the British Army's senior officer, Field Marshal

---

4   The eight-minute film can be viewed on the Imperial War Museum
    Website: https://www.iwm.org.uk/collections/item/object/1060036573

Bernard Montgomery and Dwight Eisenhower, who was Supreme Commander of the Allied Expeditionary Force in Europe and future President of the United States of America. They arrived at Tenby Station and were whisked away by military convoy to Pembroke Dock to watch rehearsals for the D-Day landings.

THE ROLE OF WOMEN

The Second World War opened up new roles for women in addition to running households, with so many men away in the armed forces. From 1941, women were called up for war work as munitions workers, air-raid wardens, mechanics, engineers and bus drivers. The Women's Land Army (WLA), originally formed in 1917, was revived in 1939 and focused on women's contribution to agriculture. Despite having little to no farming experience, these Land Girls did whatever was necessary to keep Britain self-sufficient.

Winifred Evans worked on several Pembrokeshire farms as a Land Girl, where she milked cows, ploughed fields and gathered the harvest. She lived with a farming family, while others were accommodated in hostels.

Nationally, the WLA had 80,000 members at its peak in 1943, with a sizeable number working the farms of Pembrokeshire. Lesser known were the Lumber Jills, who felled trees, stripped bark, operated sawmills and surveyed woodland in the Women's Timber Corps (WTC), formed in 1942. All recruits were subject to a medical examination to ensure that they were physically strong enough and they took a basic mathematics examination for the measurement skills that the work demanded.

PRISONERS OF WAR

When the war ended in Europe in May 1945, both the local and national authorities faced logistical challenges. These included the demobilisation of troops and what action to take with prisoners of war.

Pembrokeshire had detained Italians, many captured in northern Africa, but the arrival of German prisoners from America meant a new camp was constructed in Haverfordwest. Laws that prevented local women from fraternising were not relaxed until 1947. Local historian Mark Muller relates how prisoner Hans Pilawa was permitted to marry Mary Owen at the registry office, following which he had to return to the camp, although he was later allowed to ring his new wife to wish her goodnight. The Germans were repatriated by the end of the year.

14

PEMBROKESHIRE
AFTER 1945

In 1960, Desmond Donnelly, the MP for Pembroke, set out before Parliament the 'very grave' position facing his constituency. He described how in the immediate post-war years, the fall in demand for shipbuilding and repairing created a huge strain on the local economy.

However, hopes were raised by the advent of the super tanker and the oil industry's development around the Haven in the 1960s and 1970s. Esso's oil refinery was built on the northern shores and a landing stage for British Petroleum was constructed on the southern shores. Oil was piped to Llandarcy, 60 miles away. Such developments meant, in Donnelly's assessment, that 'the only people unemployed in the area were those who were unemployable'.

Unfortunately, the temporary nature of construction work meant that unemployment figures rose sharply. In the course of 1960, unemployment in Milford Haven had increased from 2 per cent to 11.6 per cent. Donnelly pointed out that any industrial development should be confined to the area so that the county could concentrate on tourism, which was key to Pembrokeshire's economic growth.

THE RISE OF TOURISM

Over subsequent decades, this proved an accurate prediction. Around 7 million or so tourists visit Pembrokeshire and 12,000 people are directly employed in the tourism industry, which accounts for more than one in five of the county's working population. The reopening of businesses following the Covid pandemic witnessed a significant increase in the self-catering and camping sectors. Overall, a Welsh Government audit in October 2020 reported that south-west Wales had capitalised well on the strong demand for 'staycations', far more than the south-east of the country.

The establishment of the Pembrokeshire Coast National Park in 1952, the only coastal one in the UK, was key to expanding the tourist industry although its coastal path did not open until 1970. The 186-mile trail attracts regular visitors every year. It is divided into four main sections: the south coast (Amroth–Tenby) is mainly of the bucket-and-spade nature; the stretch around Milford Haven takes in its oil refineries before approaching Angle; the west coastline covers the Marloes peninsula, looking out over St Bride's Bay to St Davids Head; and finally, the north coast runs from two key religious landmarks, St Davids Cathedral to St Dogmael's Abbey.

By 2001, only 7 per cent of Pembrokeshire people worked in agriculture, forestry and fishing combined. There are several reasons for this change. Over the years, there has been a shift from pastoral (cattle rearing) to arable farming, which calls for less labour. Technologies such as combine harvesters have also lessened the need for manual workers. (As an aside, Ian Mortimer cites the anecdote of retired farmers in another rural county – Somerset – who in the early 1960s debated which invention was the most impactful in their farming lives. They agreed it was not the tractor, electric fences or fertilisers but the wellington boot. Sometimes, lives are impacted not by the dramatic events but small changes which improve the comfort, speed or efficiency of work.) At a macro level, overseas competition and cheap food policies have seen smaller profit margins acting as a disincentive for farmers. Overfishing has led to quotas and reduced stocks, which has hit the fishing industry hard.

The development of tourism has proved something of a lifeline for farmers as they seek new income streams in the face of a series of challenges, ranging from European directives on milk quotas to outbreaks of disease such as bovine TB. In 1986, dairy farmer William McNamara opened a small family leisure park at Canaston Bridge to supplement the family income. From a low-key venture tailored mainly to BMX bikes and go-karts, by the mid 1990s Oakwood Theme Park had become a major attraction, largely due to the installation of Megafobia, rated among the best roller coasters in Europe. McNamara went on to open Bluestone National Park Resort in 2008, recognising the need to offer year-round holiday accommodation and undercover attractions in purpose-built lodges. By 2022 with around 800 employees, Bluestone had become the second biggest employer in the county, only behind the oil refinery.

Farmers have diversified in other ways – for example, through holiday lets and in supplying organic root vegetables and brassicas for niche markets. As one farmer put it, 'We cannot live by milk and lamb alone.' In 2022, more than forty Pembrokeshire farms offered accommodation with such opportunities as milking cows, pulling carrots, collecting eggs and feeding the animals.

The modern Pembrokeshire tourism industry is geared up to providing wide-ranging adventures, from foraging for edible plants and dining at the UK's first insect restaurant to walking the Tree Tops Trail or participating in the many water-based adventures such as sea kayaking, powerboating, diving, surfing and coasteering. Visit Pembrokeshire, the county's official website for tourism information, is a highly recommended starting point for up-to-date information (see the Useful Websites section of this book).

ALTERNATIVE LIFESTYLES

Since the 1960s, West Wales has seen a continual influx of those seeking alternative lives away from urbanised, industrialised existences. In 1964, the environmentalist and broadcaster John Seymour bought a seventeenth-century farm in Pembrokeshire, where he remained until his death in 2004. He wrote more than forty books supporting traditional skills and crafts, organic farming and local, small-scale economics. He opposed intensive farming practices, genetically modified crops and multinationals. He became known as the 'Father of Self Sufficiency', although as the travel writer Peter Sager discovered when he interviewed

Philip Layton, Seymour's son-in-law, 'it was his wife [Sally] who did all the work. John just wrote about it!'

The 1970s brought the so-called 'hippie' invasion, although this was more prominent in neighbouring Ceredigion. Hippies bought dilapidated cottages and smallholdings with a view to living off the land. Some individuals also participated in peace protests, such as those held at Greenham Common. In more recent times, Lammas Ecovillage near Crymych is a collective of smallholdings and eco-dwellings where residents explore alternative models for living on the land. This is broadly in line with the Welsh Government's 'One Planet Development' policy. The emphasis is on combining traditional farming and building techniques with the latest innovations in environmental design, green technology and permaculture.

THE ENERGY QUESTION

The modern oil industry in Pembrokeshire owes its origins to the expanding demand for oil in the 1950s, as car ownership increased alongside growing oil demands to fuel domestic heating and railway engines. From 1960, four refineries were built along Milford Haven, operated by Esso, British Petroleum, Gulf Oil and AMOCO. It was not long, however, before the markets changed – to the detriment of the Pembrokeshire industry.

The oil crisis of the 1970s led to a dramatic increase in prices, which reduced demand for fuel oil although petrol remained steady. The development of the North Sea gas fields presented a blow to Pembrokeshire because it offered light crude oil yielding less fuel oil in the refining process. The upshot of this was the closure of smaller refineries across Europe but there was also investment in more efficient refining technologies at the larger plants. Still, by 1998 only two of the four Milford refineries remained. And through the 1980s and 1990s, Pembrokeshire witnessed among the highest levels of unemployment in the UK.

The late twentieth and early twenty-first centuries have witnessed growing interest in renewable energy technologies, drawing power from the wind, sun and sea, in efforts to reduce carbon dioxide emissions. In 2006, a study commissioned by the

Welsh Government concluded that Pembrokeshire has the highest concentration of wave resources in Wales. Hence, there has been both local and national investment in the Pembrokeshire Demonstration Zone, which aims to demonstrate the feasibility of floating offshore wind.

Studies indicate that hydrogen could play a key role in providing low-carbon heating in homes. These developments are significant, given national targets of net zero greenhouse gas emissions by 2050. Another step towards achieving this is the requirement by 2025 for all private housing developers to reach the highest energy efficiency standards to reduce carbon use during builds and when buildings are inhabited. These changes are timely in the wake of the Covid-19 pandemic, which saw a major shift towards learning and working from home and it is forecast that this may prove a trend of the future.

Interest in solar power saw Wales's first solar park open in 2011 on the Rhosygilwen estate (at Cilgerran) with 10,000 panels which generate enough energy to power the estate. Photovoltaic (PV) solar panels are now a common sight around the county, featuring in domestic homes, public buildings and schools. Businesses such as Ty Solar have built homes in Boncath powered by solar energy.

The Pembrokeshire Coast National Park's Sustainable Development Fund focuses on supporting projects which reduce carbon and help tackle the climate emergency. In 2021, for example, Hubberston and Hakin Community Centre received a grant to install batteries to complement existing PV solar panels.

Much has been made of climate change over recent decades and it is easy to overlook the fact that through time this is a natural process. The difference, of course, is that the increasing speed of change accelerated by human activities is now being measured over years and decades rather than millennia. Most forecasters suggest that unless climate change is immediately addressed, the environmental impact on Pembrokeshire is likely to involve stronger, fiercer storms through the year, with some species unable to cope with rapid changes, crops affected by wet summers and changing seasons, for example, an earlier spring. These are not just academic points. In practical terms, fewer tourists are likely to visit seaside resorts such as Tenby in the summer, if rainy days become the norm. This has a knock-on effect for hoteliers, restaurateurs and others in the tourist industry. Employment is likely to suffer and household incomes will fall.

To get a sense of the physical change, the Pembrokeshire Coast National Park website hosts a 'Changing Coasts' map. This illustrates the erosion of cliffs and dunes, changes in vegetation, pebble banks, stream courses and flooding.[5] The general public is also invited to contribute by taking and sharing photographs at specified points to create time-lapse films to demonstrate the changes. This brings home the reality of global climate change.

One of the challenges facing the Pembrokeshire authorities is balancing the need for renewable energy sources against the economic and environmental trade-off, for example, in terms of cost and reliability, the threat to wildlife (for example, birds and bats) and visual pollution.

In 2010 Pembrokeshire County Councillors narrowly approved (by nine votes to eight) the building of Wear Point wind farm at Milford Haven. An independent study commissioned by the Welsh Government in 2014 reported that the majority of people support wind farm development and there was no evidence that they deter tourists. People are more inclined to oppose the erection of electricity pylons than wind turbines. In Pembrokeshire, another wind turbine site was erected in 2020 at Prouts Park Farm, East Williamston, while the ambitious Erebus project commenced in 2021. This represents Wales's first floating wind farm, 44km off the Pembrokeshire coast, with the capacity to power 90,000 homes. Incidentally, the project is named after a Royal Navy vessel built at Pembroke Dock in 1826. Unfortunately, in 1845 the *Erebus* became icebound on a trip to the Arctic, with total loss of life, and the wreck was not discovered until 2014.

The growing demand for renewable energy has left the Milford Haven Port Authority in a transitional phase, as it navigates from traditional support for the oil and gas industries. Its assets include an established supply chain and proximity to the Celtic Sea. There is growing political support for a move away from fossil fuels, which raises questions over the future of Pembrokeshire's oil and gas industry.

5　https://www.pembrokeshirecoast.wales/get-involved/changing-coasts/

In 2018, the Welsh Secretary Alun Cairns announced on his visit to the Valero Pembroke Refinery that the oil industry 'has the full support of the UK government'. Three years later, the Welsh Government was among those who signed the Beyond Oil and Gas Declaration, to ensure a 'managed phase out of oil and gas'. The global rise in energy prices, coupled with uncertainty over supply due to the Ukraine conflict in 2022, has produced a cost of living crisis that has become a major policy challenge at local and national level.

The regional and national economic uncertainty has been compounded by Covid-19 and the withdrawal of the UK from the European Union (Brexit) in 2020. Forecasters suggest that counties such as Pembrokeshire, which are characterised by an elderly population, an economic reliance on tourism and hospitality, and with pockets of significant social deprivation, are most at risk. Pembrokeshire also has high proportions of self-employed people, seasonal workers who face underemployment and those in low-paid jobs, while its main towns are generally in economic decline.

Pembrokeshire County Council's Recovery and Regeneration Strategy 2020–30 sees the potential of the county becoming 'the green energy capital of the UK'. This revolves around such initiatives as the Pembroke Dock Marine Development and securing Milford Haven as a freeport (with tax relief benefits) to safeguard existing jobs and support moves towards renewable energy.

In recent years, another challenge facing Pembrokeshire's councillors is the revitalising of its towns in the face of online shopping habits and the growth of out-of-town retail parks. Hence, there have been attempts to reimagine towns, not just as shopping centres but as enterprise hubs and cultural attractions. For example, 'The LAB Haverfordwest', supported by the Arts Council of Wales, aims to change perceptions of the town by reconnecting with its river and showcasing the role of the arts in bringing the community together.

15

PEMBROKESHIRE ARTS

Artists have long been attracted to Pembrokeshire, inspired by its landscape and coastline. As the Angle-born artist, poet and sculptor Bob Reaves points out, 'The glory of Pembrokeshire is that the next stop is Mexico.'

The Yorkshire draughtsman Francis Place produced one of the earliest sketches of the Pembrokeshire coast during a drawing and angling tour of 1678. Unfortunately, Place had the misfortune of being arrested, along with his fellow artist William Lodge, on suspicion of being Jesuit spies. These were tense times, with suspected Catholic plots to assassinate Charles II, so the presence of any stranger studying and drawing coastal defences, castles and quaysides was likely to arouse suspicion.

This did not prevent John Attwood from depicting the Royal Navy ships at Milford Haven, although this was not painted until around 1776. This is his only known work, which is of considerable value for marine historians.

In the nineteenth century, Pembrokeshire produced a string of artists, including Thomas George from Fishguard, whose miniatures were exhibited at the Royal Academy. Penally's Benjamin Phelps Gibbon was a line engraver, who included Queen Victoria among his subjects. James Milo sculptured the bronze statue of Sir Hugh Owen, pioneer of higher education in Wales, which stands outside Caernarvon Castle.

The etcher Charles Norris moved from Norwich to Tenby in about 1805 and worked in Pembrokeshire until his death in 1858. Most of his work comprises sketches, notably of Tenby, St Davids and Pembroke. His most famous work, *Etchings of Tenby* was published in 1812; a digitised version can be viewed on the National Library of Wales website.

War with France meant that it was dangerous for artists to travel to the continent from about 1780 to 1815. Hence, many looked to the Welsh landscape as an alternative to the Alps. The most famous visitor was J.M.W. Turner, who made his first tour in 1792. His painting of *Pembroke Castle* (*c*.1829) shows fishermen unloading their catch from a boat moored on the beach, oblivious to the imposing castle in the background.

The Pre-Raphaelite artist John Brett considered Pembrokeshire was 'the only one really satisfactory seaside place on the whole British coast'. His most famous works include *Skag Rock, Pembrokeshire* (1879) and *The Isles of Skomer and Skokholm* (1891). The Pre-Raphaelites aimed to capture nature as accurately as possible, often painting outside. Brett's painting of *Forest Cove* (1883), to the east of Dinas Head, has been used to estimate the rate of coastal change in Fishguard Bay.

In the twentieth century, the Pembrokeshire seaside continued to fascinate artists. Tenby's Augustus and Gwen John are discussed later. Anglesey-born Kyffin Williams, one of Britain's greatest landscape painters, produced many Pembrokeshire seascapes during a long career. In 2019, more than 11,000 visitors attended an exhibition at Haverfordwest's new cultural centre which showcased his work.

Williams considered John Piper, who worked as an official artist at the Ministry of War Transport, an honorary Welshman and praised him for trying to see what hadn't been seen before. Among Piper's works is *Coast of Pembroke*, painted between 1938 and 1940.

David Jones, a poet and artist, was fascinated by the ever-changing sea and used this a metaphor for creativity. In his 1925 watercolour *Tenby from Caldey Island*, he contrasts the island's monastic calmness with the mainland buzz of people and shipping. Jones turned to Caldey to help him come to terms with his experiences in the trenches of the Great War.

The London artist Graham Sutherland acknowledged that he learnt to paint in Pembrokeshire after his first visit in 1934. He returned every year until 1945 and again between 1967 and his death in 1980. Sutherland was attracted, like so many other artists, to the quality of light. His *Estuary with Rocks* (1937–38) was inspired by his time at Sandy Haven. Sutherland donated 300 or so of his paintings for display at Picton Castle 'he decided that work done in a certain area is seen best in that area'.

In north Pembrokeshire, Jenny Keal's *Nevern Estuary* hints at the human relationship with the landscape and the impact of the weather and geology of the mountains, valleys and coast. John Knapp-Fisher deliberately uses a limited palette to explore 'the edge of colour' to paint powerful pieces, such as *Derraint's Cottage*, which are often dark in atmosphere. In contrast, Annabel Greenhalgh's use of pastel conveys an uplifting feeling, as in *Summer's Evening, Freshwater West* or *Path to Druidston*.

Pembrokeshire's appeal to artists is that it offers a diversity of landscape, seascape, rivers, valleys, hidden cottages, working farms, abandoned industrial sites and the Preseli Hills, all of which change with the seasons. Vanessa Pearson's work is based on the premise that her best, most dynamic results are achieved by painting on the spot rather than copying from photographic material, which only captures an image frozen in time devoid of movement or light. Sitting outside may not always be the most comfortable experience, but it enables her to directly experience the elements and her spontaneous reaction to the subject, whether painting primroses, sleeping sheep or Pembroke Castle.

16

PORTS AND LIGHTHOUSES

Pembrokeshire has three main commercial ports (Fishguard, Pembroke Dock and Milford Haven) and several smaller private ones, along with eight lighthouses. They are key to its maritime operations, heritage and economy.

In the sixteenth century, Tenby was a prominent Pembrokeshire port. A survey of 1566 said the port could accommodate ships of 300 tons at all tides. The same survey suggested that in the area of Milford there were nineteen landing places in addition to the port. The main exports were wheat, oats, corn and rye but other grains, such as malt (for beer), were also imported, depending upon the success of the harvests. These fluctuated – for example, 1586 was exceptionally poor, but 1592 was a very good one.

The first Pembrokeshire lighthouse was built at St Ann's Head High in 1714. Others include those located on the Smalls (1775); Caldey Island (1829); South Bishop (1839); St Ann's Head Low (1841); Saundersfoot (1848); Pembroke Dock (unknown); Newton Noyes (unknown); Little Castle Head and Great Castle Head (both around 1870); Middle Channel Rock (unknown); Watwick Point (unknown); West Blockhouse Point (unknown); Pen Anglas (unknown); Fishguard North Breakwater (1905); East Breakwater (unknown); Strumble Head (1908); and Skokholm (around 1915). The major coastal lighthouses are maintained by Trinity House in Harwich (Essex), the British lighthouse administrative body.

The South Bishop lighthouse, on what was formerly called Emsger (Norse for 'isolated rock at sea'), off St Davids Head, was erected in the path of migrating birds. Unfortunately, many were dazzled by the brilliance of the light at night which led them to dash themselves against the lantern. Special bird perches were placed outside the lantern which reduced the number of strikes.

The lamp at the Smalls Lighthouse, which is about 20 miles off St Ann's Head, is at one of the most exposed positions in the whole of the British Isles. According to Fenton, the original lighthouse was constructed in 1775 by a certain 'H. Whitesides' (although his surname had no 's'), an engineer living in Solva. It was at the bequest of a Liverpool merchant named John Phillips, a native of Cardiganshire.

The design was based on eight pillars of iron with wooden supports – but the storms in the first winter were so strong that the joints and bolts were loosened. Henry Whiteside decided to put his own work to the test by occupying the lighthouse and experiencing the trials of winter for himself.

In February 1777, Fenton describes how Whiteside, who was short of drinking water and lacked a fire, cast three messages into the sea in corked bottles directed to Thomas Williams, who acted as the agent for John Phillips. One of the bottles landed in Galway Bay, another on Newgale Sands but the third, as luck would have it, was washed ashore at a creek close to the home of Thomas Williams at Trelethin near St Davids.

Fenton secured and reprinted a copy of the letter in the bottle, in which Whiteside 'prayeth for your immediate assistance to fetch us off the Smalls before next spring, or we fear we shall all perish'. The story had a happy ending as all were rescued and Whiteside was able to correct the early faults.

However, not all tales were so uplifting. In 1801, one of the two lighthouse keepers, Thomas Griffith, fell ill and died. His colleague, Thomas Howell, feared that he would be blamed for his death. As a former joiner, he used his skills to make a coffin in which the corpse was placed and then stored it on a shelf outside the lighthouse, so he did not have to see the body. However, the coffin was soon battered by the extreme weather and one of the corpse's arms stretched out to torment Howells.

Ships that passed by were oblivious to the torment. It was only after the storms ceased that a supply boat from Milford on a routine journey to the island discovered one dead body and one broken man.

In 1885, the lighthouse was rebuilt and 100 or so years later it became fully automated. In 2016, the story was turned into a film directed by Chris Crow called *The Lighthouse*, starring Mark Lewis Jones.

17

SHIPWRECKS

Despite the best efforts of lighthouse keepers, over the centuries storms off the Pembrokeshire coastline have wrecked hundreds of ships and resulted in significant loss of life. The website Dive Pembrokeshire has a comprehensive listing, with most of the wrecks remaining undiscovered.[6]

Some can be visited by scuba divers – diving around the cable-laying *Behar*, for example, brings into sight conga eels and octopuses amid the Harley Davidson bikes and artillery that formed part of the cargo when the ship sank in 1940.

It was common for thieves to take advantage of shipwrecks, pilfering washed-ashore cargo before officials arrived. Occasionally, however, they got more than they bargained for. In 1791, the *Increase* was driven ashore in St Bride's Bay carrying a cargo of condemned gunpowder from the British garrison in the West Indies. The crew and a single lady passenger were safely helped ashore with their possessions.

The following morning, plunderers smashed open the barrels of gunpowder to seize the valuable copper hoops that bound them. It wasn't long before the sand and nearby rocks were smothered in powder.

One of the pillagers snatched a musket and foolishly threw it against a rock, which in turn caused a spark that set off a chain of explosions among the scattered gunpowder. One young woman was immediately killed and seven others died later from their injuries, while more than sixty were badly hurt. The local Rector of Nolton, who observed the carnage, wrote, 'The cliffs resounded with the groans of the sufferers, with the lamentations

---

6   http://www.dive-pembrokeshire.com

and eager inquiries of fathers for their children, of husbands for
their wives, of brothers for sisters, of children for their parents.'
He had little sympathy, however, claiming that it was an act of
God, punishing them for their wickedness. Despite the incident,
looting continued until the local militia arrived. Those arrested
were eventually acquitted.

Before the introduction of shipping forecasts in 1924, seafarers
relied on their own skills in predicting the weather based on the
movement of the clouds, the state of the sea, wind direction and
the behaviour of fish, sea mammals and birds. Any sign of major
change would force mariners to seek refuge in the nearest harbour,
hence the saying 'any port in a storm'.

The most dramatic recorded event was the Great Storm of
1703, in which a week-long hurricane caused havoc. Daniel Defoe
wrote *The Storm* based on eyewitness accounts. These included a
letter from Captain Joseph Soanes, who was in charge of about
130 merchant ships at Milford Haven. On 27 November, Soanes
observed with the coming of daylight the horror of 'ships without

The × denotes the spot where the Loch Shiel was wrecked.

Figs. 22 A map showing the location of the Loch Shiel wreck, while custom
officials searched for missing whiskey barrels in the area.

masts, some sunk, and others upon the rocks, the wind blowing so hard, with thunder, lightning, and rain, that on the deck a man could not stand'. More than thirty ships were lost in the night.

The storm of October 1859 also caused major havoc. The most devastating loss of life occurred when the *Royal Charter* was wrecked off Anglesey, claiming 459 lives. It is described vividly by Charles Dickens in *The Uncommercial Traveller*.

Along the Pembrokeshire coast there were many small schooners which ran aground. The *Charles Holmes* had a crew of twenty-eight and one passenger, all of whom perished. The cargo consisted of coal, iron, tools, clothing and crockery, much of which was blown ashore at Aberbach.

The storms of November 1866 forced one ship after another onto the rocks at St Ann's Head. Unfortunately, when the first two ships ran aground their lights were mistaken by other ships as the lights of Dale Roads, a safe anchorage. Five ships were subsequently wrecked with few reported survivors.

Perhaps the most famous of Pembrokeshire's shipwreck stories is the fate of the schooner *Loch Shiel*. In January 1894 it set off with a cargo of 100 per cent proof whisky and gunpowder bound for Australia. The crew struggled to make headway against strong winds and were forced inshore, where she struck rocks below Thorn Island just before midnight (Figure 22).

As the pumps failed to keep out the water, a mattress was set alight on deck as an emergency distress signal and the Angle lifeboat came to the rescue. Such quick thinking saved the lives of those on board.

The coxswain of the Angle lifeboat was awarded the Royal National Lifeboat Institution (RNLI) silver medal for rescuing thirty of the crew. However, as the ship broke up, wooden cases of whisky were washed ashore, much to the delight of the Angle villagers who hid their loot – although one man died from drinking too much. Two bottles remained concealed until they were discovered during the renovation of a cottage in 1950.

There are stories that unscrupulous individuals waved lanterns in the evenings along the cliff edges near Marloes to lure ships onto the rocks, and even of lanterns being tied under the necks of cows or horses' tails. However, there are doubts because cows are far too sensible to hover on the edge of a steep cliff on stormy nights.

In Marloes, another tale relates how the preacher interrupted his own sermon on hearing the news of a particular wreck and asked the congregation to 'wait a moment, my brethren, and give your pastor a fair start!'

THE RNLI IN PEMBROKESHIRE

The RNLI was established in 1824, although the earliest Welsh lifeboat station predates this. The Fishguard station was founded in 1822 and became a member of the RNLI in 1855. Other stations soon opened around the Pembrokeshire coast, including Tenby, in 1852, and St Davids in 1869. The bravery, courage and self-sacrifice of the lifeboat crews have saved many lives along the Pembrokeshire coast (Figure 23).

The lifeboats were operated by volunteers who needed considerable strength, courage and teamwork skills in the highly risky business of saving lives. Tenby's extreme tidal range meant that the lifeboat had to be dragged 2½ miles across the beach when the tide was low before it could be launched into the sea and then had to be hauled back up the slope afterwards. One of the major challenges was getting from the shore to the sea as quickly as possible. The early launches depended on 'pulling and sailing', launched from a carriage on an open beach. In 1896, it was reported that 106 people had turned up to assist with a single launch in Tenby.

Wheeled carriages and horses provided some assistance, along with volunteers, who were entitled to a reward. This incentive brought large crowds. A holidaymaker in 1854 described how he saw a great crowd gather at the quay and people eagerly running through the streets to join them:

> Seven or eight young fellows were putting on jackets made of parallel strips of cork bound together. Presently three or four of them jump overboard, and being of course sufficiently buoyant in their cork armour, play rude frolics in the water.

The boat was then deliberately upended, adding authenticity and challenge, while the rescue party used another 'lighter' with ropes attached to upturn it.

The first Welsh lifeboat to be powered by an internal combustion engine was the *Charterhouse* from Fishguard in 1908. There were other improvements. Horse-drawn carriages were replaced by boathouses and purpose-built slipways – the Tenby Lifeboat House opened on Castle Hill in 1905, jutting out into deeper water with a 365ft slipway, which is the second largest in Britain after Weston-super-Mare. The weekly test launches remain a popular attraction for tourists and locals. In 2010 the station was converted into a house after a third station opened in 2006.

The growth of tourism since the 1950s has required a different kind of emergency response, with attention focusing more on helping struggling swimmers, coastal walkers cut off by the tide or drifting dinghies than large merchant vessels in distress. Navigational aids have come a long way since the chronometer, compass and sextant. Nowadays, stations are equipped with satellite technologies that pinpoint ships' locations and courses.

Fig. 23 Nineteenth-century print of a lifeboat crew.

18

BEACHES

Pembrokeshire boasts outstanding beaches which vary considerably in their terrain. There are regular reports of its beaches winning accolades. In 2022, for example, Barafundle Bay was named as one of the UK's most photogenic picnic spots. In total eleven beaches were awarded Blue Flag status. This is awarded by an international panel of environmentalists, conservationists and lifesavers, who examine samples of seawater on a regular basis, organised through the Keep Wales Tidy organisation. The award recognises high standards of cleanliness and good overall beach management. Among the criteria are the presence of lifeguards or lifesaving and first aid equipment, access to toilets, drinking water and public information displays, such as maps, natural history information and up-to-date details of local water quality. The Blue Flag is only awarded for the duration of one season to maintain standards.

Pembrokeshire also has small, wild beaches such as the shingle cove at Porthsychan, Marloes Sands and Albion Sands, named after a paddle steamer which ran aground in 1837. These are recognised by an additional scheme, Keep Wales Tidy's Green Coast Awards. These acknowledge the excellent water quality and unspoiled environment, without the infrastructure and intensive management generally associated with more traditional seaside resorts.

Saundersfoot's Blue Flag beach is ideal for small children to enjoy paddling, with lots of amenities nearby. The golden sands of Broad Haven North have been a favourite destination since the 1800s when bathing machines first appeared. During low tide, it's possible to walk around the headland to the village of Little Haven. In contrast, the pebbly Blue Flag beach at Dale is ideal for watersports and is a favourite spot for windsurfers.

Rip currents are particularly dangerous. They can move at a rate of 4.5mph, which is faster than an Olympic swimmer. The RNLI advice if caught in a rip current is:

> Don't panic or try to swim against it. If you can, stand and wade. If you can't stand, swim parallel to the shore, raise your hand and shout for help.

There are occasional news stories of individuals caught out by rip currents, which can lead to tragic consequences. Hence, it is important to be familiar with what each flag means and to follow RNLI guidance:

- Red flag – danger, do not go into the water.
- Red and white prohibition sign – do not enter the water.
- Red and yellow sign – lifeguarded area for swimming, bodyboarding and using inflatables.
- No lifeguards sign – this beach is not lifeguarded. You can still enter the water but do so at your own risk.
- Orange flag – indicates offshore or strong wind – do not use inflatables.
- Black and white sign – area for surfing and using any other non-powered craft. Recovery area. No swimming or bodyboarding.

COASTEERING

Coasteering describes the traversing of the coast by a combination of climbing, cliff jumping and swimming. Such adrenalin-filled activities are promoted as opportunities to discover areas which are normally inaccessible, providing remote relaxation in contrast to the more conventional 'quiet enjoyment' pastimes of walking, nature-watching and angling. Companies such as Celtic Quest Coasteering offer cliff jumping, adventure swimming and scramble climbing for those over the age of 8. The challenge for the Pembrokeshire National Park authorities is to preserve the special features of the park and its tranquillity while promoting opportunities for adventure.

19

PEMBROKESHIRE TOWNS

Pembrokeshire is essentially a rural county with only ten towns and the cathedral city of St Davids. Four of the towns were created in the nineteenth century: Milford Haven was developed as a port; Pembroke Dock was a dockyard for the Royal Navy; Neyland became the terminus for Isambard Kingdom Brunel's South Wales Railway and Saundersfoot grew to meet the needs of the local colliery and ironworks. These supplemented the older castle towns at Pembroke, Haverfordwest, Newport, Tenby and Narberth, along with the historic port at Fishguard.

FISHGUARD

Fishguard as a town was established in the tenth century, probably as a Viking trading post. Its Welsh name, *Abergwaun*, means 'Mouth of the River Gwaun'. Through the Middle Ages, Lower Fishguard developed as a herring fishing port. One story suggests that supplies became so abundant that the herrings were spread across the fields of West Wales as a form of fertiliser.

As a port, Fishguard needed protection. During the American War of Independence, the French (as American allies) encouraged attacks on British ships. In 1779, the American privateer Stephen Manhant anchored the *Black Prince* off the Fishguard coast and demanded payment. This was no empty threat – Manhant had already sunk thirty or so British ships in the previous three months. However, the town authorities refused to pay and exchanged cannon fire, which forced Manhant away. The incident triggered the building of Fishguard Fort to strength the town's defences.

Fishguard was the last place that a foreign army invaded Britain. In 1797, a force of 600 French soldiers and 800 convicts, despite flying British colours, were spotted off Strumble Head coast by a vigilant old sailor called Williams. On 22 February, at around ten o'clock in the morning, two frigates, a corvette and a lugger landed opposite Llanwnda, 3 miles west of Fishguard. Using his spying glass, the intrepid Williams suddenly exclaimed, 'Good God! the d***n French!'

His wife confirmed, '*Duw anwyl*! Indeed now! The French! And there they was!' At least, this was how the *Welshman* reported the story in its centenary edition of 1897. It was another woman, however, who became legendary.

Little is known about Jemima Niclas beyond her epitaph in St Mary's Church, 'The Welsh Heroine who boldly marched to meet the French invaders'. Born in Llanrhian and the 47-year-old wife of a cobbler, legend has it that Niclas, armed only with a pitchfork, led a group of women and rounded up a dozen drunken French soldiers in no condition to fight. While searching for food, they had stumbled across and consumed too much liquor which locals had 'rescued' from a shipwreck.

The women donned tall, black hats and red petticoats, which may have confused the French into thinking that they were British troops. In any event, the French party was captured and detained in the church overnight. Their leaders surrendered shortly afterwards at the Royal Oak public house, which retains memorabilia of the event.

In recognition of her efforts, Niclas was awarded a lifetime pension of £50, which she collected every year until her death at the age of 82. *The Welshman*'s centenary coverage of the invasion described 'How England was saved by the Women of Pembrokeshire'.

Following the surrender of the French, their Irish-born American commander, William Tate, was imprisoned in Dartmoor while 415 of his men were sent to Haverfordwest Gaol. While the invasion has been depicted in popular culture in a light-hearted manner, it was a serious warning to the authorities that parts of the coastline were relatively undefended.

One of the postscripts to the story was that two Welsh girls who worked in the prisons that detained the captured French soldiers fell in love with two of them. They smuggled a shinbone of beef into Pembroke Gaol and with it the prisoners patiently excavated a hole big enough to escape. The party reached the harbour to take a cargo boat to France but the tide was too low and so they seized Lord Cawdor's personal yacht and made their escape. On the 100th anniversary, in 2019, a distant relative from Australia bought a hat which is said to have belonged to Niclas for £5,000. Fishguard Library has a tapestry which tells the story of the invasion.

Historically, Fishguard held little to attract visitors other than a route to Ireland. In 1804, Benjamin Malkin described the town as 'so filthy, so ill built, and so uncivilized', pointing to the 'miserable' church and lack of schools as evidence of the people's 'negligent character'. The main streets were described as barely passable for traffic, littered with holes and dunghills – 'I do not mean mere heaps of dirt, but literal and bona fide dunghills'.

Social improvements within the town were very much linked to the economic fortunes of its port. Over the centuries, most of the trade was with Ireland and south-west England, particularly Bristol, with occasional imports of timber from faraway lands such as Canada and Sweden. During the eighteenth and nineteenth centuries, among the main exports were oats and butter. Demand for culm, which was a form of discarded, granular coal, increased steadily, which warranted the development of creeks at Landshipping, Hook and Lawrenny.

Lower Fishguard's pier and quayside were completed in 1862, with ships charged tolls on entering the harbour based on their registered tonnage. An alternative was to discharge cargo on Goodwick Beach, just below Fishguard, to avoid tolls, although this was only possible during favourable weather conditions.

In the twentieth century, the main imports were shop goods, coal and fertiliser, with occasional imports of bricks, timber and tiles. In 1906, Fishguard Harbour Station was officially opened when the Waterford and Cork ferry services were transferred from Neyland.

After 1914 trade declined, and by the 1930s the only substantial import was flour. The port of Fishguard closed in 1948. However, the link between Fishguard and Ireland was strengthened by a car ferry service to Rosslare Harbour, which was introduced in 1965. Previously, cars had been lifted off the steamers by crane and brought to the mainland on railway wagons. Nowadays, the ferry service runs two ferries a day to Rosslare, all year round.

HAVERFORDWEST

The origin of the name Haverfordwest has long been debated. John Brown suggested in his history of the town, published in 1914, that the Welsh name *Hwlffordd* combines a road, way or passage (*ffordd*) with a sort of vine (*Hwl*), which he then connected to the tradition that a vine grew in the open on the banks of the river. He attributed the 'west' element of the name to the fording spot over the western Cleddau. As to the prefix 'Haver', Brown concluded that because '*haver*' meant oats in provincial English, there was a distinct possibility that this was where the crop was brought for shipping away. Other possible explanations for the town's name are that it was a ford or crossing point for heifers or goats driven to market. Hence the name Goat Street (the Old English word *hæfer* meant a male goat). The 'west' was added by the fifteenth century to distinguish the town from Hereford.

The reference to the people of Haverfordwest as 'Long Necks' has various explanations. One suggestion is that it describes the local habit of trying to peer over the high walls of the old town gaol or union workhouse, while another tale described pavements full of men standing on tiptoe and stretching their necks to try and see into the ground where Haverfordwest played football without having to pay an entrance fee.

Haverfordwest dates its establishment as a town to 1110, when Tancred, a Flemish leader, settled and built a wooden stronghold. Its central location was accessible along the River Cleddau from Milford Haven, which allowed salt, iron, wine and apples to be imported. The Bristol Trader pub and old warehouses are reminders of a once-thriving trade.

The market functioned around St Mary's Church in medieval times and remained there until 1827, when it moved to what became Market Street. A third church, St Thomas's, had been built by the close of the thirteenth century and the presence of three Anglican churches was a sign of the town's wealth.

By the 1600s, Haverfordwest had established itself as the main town in the county. It had its own grammar school, Member of Parliament, gaol, poorhouse and shire buildings, although the present Shire Hall was not built until 1837.

Such wealth provided no comfort when plague arrived in late 1651, probably from sailors whose vessel arrived at Milford Haven. 'Pest Houses' were set aside for quarantine. Attempts were made to isolate the town by preventing exit and entry except for supplies. Shoemakers and felt makers complained that no one came to buy their goods.

Hundreds likely died in a population of 3,000, and a third fell into poverty. One of the heroes was the Reverend Stephen Lowe, Rector of St Thomas's, who collected money and provisions and visited the sick. He died in 1656, worn out. Not all efforts were well received. Plague nurses were generally viewed with suspicion, with allegations that they robbed the dying. A 'strange woman' called Joane Cheate was employed in Haverfordwest, evidently from outside the area, and was subjected to abuse.

The town became a fashionable venue for both local gentry and visitors. William Pitt the Elder, the future prime minister, arrived in 1736, the year in which he gave his maiden speech in Parliament. Pitt liked Haverfordwest as a centre for trade, although he found it was 'a devil of a town to walk in'.

The travel writer Mary Morgan held similar views in the 1790s. The main street was so poorly paved that it made her move in a manner something between sliding and walking. However, this did not detract from her overall impression. She found Haverfordwest was 'one of the most singular and pretty places you can conceive'. The whitewashed houses flanking the main street like soldiers stood in contrast to what Mary had seen on her travels in other towns, where the houses were discoloured with smoke.

Haverfordwest has long been an Anglicised town. The travel writer H.V. Morton concluded on his visit in 1932, 'You could plant it anywhere in Devon or Somerset and it would look right. There is nothing of Wales about it: even the voice of Haverfordwest is the voice of England.' Recent census figures show that less than 15 per cent of the town's population speak

Welsh. Both local and national government policy has sought to encourage the use of the Welsh language, promoting and protecting Welsh culture. This has resulted in the expansion of Welsh-medium education, including the opening in 2018 of a new Welsh-medium all-through school (3–16) in Haverfordwest.

Over recent years, regeneration plans have included a new Riverside Shopping Centre, indoor food emporium and better access to the castle. The need to redevelop the town is seen as key to its economic growth, building on its strategic value as a base from which to explore the Pembrokeshire Coast National Park and the Preseli Hills.

MILFORD HAVEN

The Haven in the town's name was added in the nineteenth century to the Norse origin in recognition of the waterway's strategic importance. In 1171, Henry II gathered his troops here as a departure point for Ireland, while in August 1405 an army of around 12,000 men on 120 ships arrived here from France to assist Owain Glyndwr in his rebellion against Henry IV. In subsequent centuries, fortifications were built around the Haven to protect shipping and deter invaders. But it was not until the late eighteenth century that Milford grew to become a town.

In 1785, a packet service carrying mail had been established linking Hubberston Hakin to Dunmore in Ireland. These were named after the mail packets of urgent correspondence delivered to and from British embassies and colonies.

The Fishguard crossing to Ireland typically took twelve hours. The travel writer Joseph Romilly and his companion made the journey in 1827, amid a violent storm, but still managed to arrive at Milford in fourteen hours. They were relieved to take in a good meal at the local inn and relax with a game of backgammon.

Milford's expansion was due to the combined efforts of Sir William Hamilton, who had married Catherine Barlow of Slebech, and his nephew, Charles Francis Greville. Hamilton wanted to develop the harbour to accommodate his trade interests and asked Greville to manage the project. Part of this involved developing a whaling fleet to serve the growing demand for street lighting, fuelled by whale oil.

Quaker families who were originally from Nova Scotia and had moved to Nantucket possessed extensive experience in the industry and were invited to relocate to West Wales. They are remembered in such names as Nantucket Avenue and Starbuck Road (Starbuck was one of the family names). Greville planned the town on a grid system with parallel streets running nearly due east and west, in the direction of the shore, intersected by shorter streets of communication at right angles.

The town was also boosted by the Navy Board's decision to contract a private company to build warships at Milford, which led to the opening of the Royal Shipyard in 1797. Admiral Horatio Nelson visited in 1802 and praised the progress of building both royal vessels and the sending of whale ships to the southern seas. Nelson regarded Milford as 'the finest and most extensive harbour in the known world'. The Lord Nelson Hotel, originally built by Sir William Hamilton in 1795 as the New Inn, was renamed after Nelson's visit. Incidentally, its ballroom was the first in the UK to be lit by electricity on 1 September 1879.

The town's fortunes changed for the worse with the transfer of the Royal Dockyard to Pembroke Dock in 1815. As he toured the town Milford (Figure 24), Roscoe described 'scores of houses shut up' and the townsfolk wandering sadly about, 'congregating in little groups, with the tacit understanding to be unhappy together'. He thought they looked like 'walking spirit of by-gone days' and pitied the hotelier's attempt to keep going.

Fortunes picked up with the opening of the Milford Docks in 1888, which provided a base for trawlers and boosted the fishing industry. By the early 1900s, several local ice factories were opened so that there was no longer a need to rely on imported Norwegian ice. In 1908, a large fish market and smokehouse with good railway connections signalled prosperous times.

By the mid-1920s, Milford Haven was in the company of Hull, Grimsby and Fleetwood as the four chief fishing ports in England and Wales. On his tour of Wales in 1932, the travel writer Henry Morton recorded the most spectacular experience of his life. Huge numbers of fish were sorted and washed at the dockside, covering an area 60,000 square feet. Buyers arrived at 8 a.m. and all sales

Fig. 24 Milford Haven (*c.*1837). (*Roscoe, 1837, plate XXXII*)

were completed by 10 a.m. He likened this to 'some weird army kit-inspection', with special trains steaming out of Milford Haven, taking fish to London, Manchester and Cardiff. Morton was most impressed by the girls 'with sturdy, bare arms', who in three strokes slit and gutted herring and had them hanging up smoking over oak chips within a few minutes. In 1946, the fishing industry was at its peak, processing 59,000 tons of herring.

The strategic importance of Milford Haven meant that the authorities were eager to ensure that it was well defended from any foreign invasion. Barracks had already been installed to guard the south side of Pembroke Dock when the Royal Commission on the Defence of the United Kingdom decided that six forts should be built around the northern part of the Haven.

Due to the cost, only one was constructed – Scoveston Fort was completed in 1864, although even then, it lacked the firepower necessary to defend the shore. A similar story of financial constraint limited developments in south Pembrokeshire when only St Catherine's Island, off Tenby, was fortified, although it never saw action.

Back at Milford, further defences were constructed including an electrified minefield, while the concrete Chapel Bay Battery Fort was added in the 1880s. During the First World War, an anti-sub-marine boom and net were added between Dale and Thorn Island. Submarine warfare had already been explored in the 1870s when a base was established at East Pennar Point to test and develop new technologies such as torpedoes. Testing of underwater weapons continued until 1905, when the depot closed.

During the Second World War, Milford Haven was chosen as a base for Allied American troops and other personnel, 1,000 of whom were housed in the town during the war. Despite many German bombing raids, Milford escaped any serious damage.

In the post-war period, the fishing industry declined because of over-fishing and competition from elsewhere, but the economy received an important boost when Esso opened the first oil refinery in 1960. Others followed, and by the early 1980s Esso was the second largest oil refinery in the UK. The Milford Marina opened in 1991 and has since seen the waterfront development of various shops, restaurants and the Milford Haven Museum, housed in the Old Customs House.

NARBERTH

Today, Narberth is one of the trendier places in the county, described by the journalist Tony Curtis as 'the Cowbridge of Pembrokeshire'. In 2020, its independent shops along the High Street contributed to the town being voted the best place to live in Wales by the *Sunday Times*. However, the lockdowns associated with Covid-19, the rise of online shopping and the ongoing cost-of-living crisis has squeezed independent traders on high streets up and down the land.

The town was first mentioned as 'Arberth' in the medieval Welsh folk tales, *Y Mabinogion* (properly, *Mabinogi*), meaning 'tales of youth'. It was the chief court of Pwyll, who ruled the region. The *Mabinogi* mattered, particularly, in an age when few could read or write. Bards composed poetry and songs in celebration of their patron's achievements, or simply to entertain. They would adapt their stories as they travelled around, for example by changing names, to suit new patrons or locations.

In the town centre there is a museum and an old hotel named after Baron de Rutzen, a Latvian who owned the Slebech estate by marriage in 1822. Rutzen ran into difficulties with the Bishop of St Davids, who brought court action against him because Rutzen had pulled down Minwear Church without the bishop's permission. The church had fallen into disrepair and Rutzen decided to use the communion table in his farmhouse and the font as a pig trough, which annoyed locals and was seen as sacrilegious. The court ordered that the church be restored.

The town hall was built in 1835 and is the most striking building in the High Street. There is also an art gallery called Oriel Q, which hosts regular exhibitions and workshops.

NEWPORT

The town lays in the shadow of Carn Ingli, with its 'Sleeping Giant' of three rocky outcrops said to be guarding the townspeople. The Welsh name, *Trefdraeth*, means 'town by the beach'. The 'new' in the English name is misleading because this is one of the oldest settlements in the county – Mesolithic remains have been discovered near the bridge.

Anglo-Norman lords held power in the district, channelled through their castle at Nevern. In 1191, William Martin relocated a few miles west, establishing a new castle, town and port, hence the name, Newport. The port became an important centre for trade in wool, herring and pottery, while the castle has been a private dwelling for more than 150 years. Its locational significance is borne out by the fact that two Welsh leaders, Llewelyn the Great and later Owain Glyndwr, fought to capture it from the Normans.

A new quay was established at the Parrog, following changes in the silting of the estuary. This provided shipbuilding facilities, storehouses and limekilns. Newport has the most complete fifteenth-century kiln in the UK, which can be seen behind protective glass at the side of the Memorial Hall. The word 'kiln' comes from the old Welsh word '*cylyn*', meaning 'cooking stove' or 'burning place'. However, this was no ordinary kiln. Local historian Tom Bennett reckons it could fire 1,300 pots in one session.

The church of St Mary's was rebuilt in the nineteenth century but retains its original thirteenth-century tower and is a grade-II-listed building. Among the oldest pubs is the Golden Lion, originally called the Green Dragon, which was mentioned in the 1790s.

Newport was the location of the ancient game of Cnapan which was played during Easter. Cnapan was the name of a ball the size of a clenched fist. The game essentially involved neighbouring parish teams attempting to transfer the ball into the church of one's home parish by any means possible. Cnapan could descend into wrestling, brawling and violence with several deaths reported from stabbing. It represented a free-for-all, mass-participation sport. George Owen, writing in 1603, described the scene:

> It is oftentimes seen the chase to follow two miles and more. It is a strange sight to see a thousand or fifteen hundred naked men to concur together in a cluster in following the cnapan as the same is hurled backward and forward.

Between the mid-1980s and 1990s a refereed version of the game was revived between Nevern and Newport parishioners but was abandoned due to the difficulties in obtaining insurance cover for participants. In modern times, the town's Cnapan Guest House along with holiday lets vie for the tourist trade which is attracted by the beach, coastal walks, golf, kayaking and other adventures.

NEYLAND

Before the mid-nineteenth century, Neyland was a small village of about 200 inhabitants. In the eighteenth century, a shipyard had been built to supply warships for the wars with France. The modern town was formed in 1856 when the South Wales Railway was extended from Haverfordwest to Neyland.

In 1858, the railway company opened an overseas steam route to Portugal and Brazil. Thereafter the town was also known as New Milford, at least until 1906 when the invaluable Irish traffic transferred to Fishguard.

The great engineer Isambard Kingdom Brunel had surveyed the Haven in 1851 on board the *Cambria* steamer. He is thus regarded as the founder of Neyland, and this is commemorated by a bronze statue of him erected in 1999. It showed him holding a steam locomotive in one hand and the *Great Eastern* in the other. In 2013 a replacement Brunel statue was unveiled, funded by local residents after the original was stolen.

The *Great Eastern* was the world's biggest ship at the time, with a capacity of 4,000 passengers, which arrived in Neyland in 1860 from New York. It was not a simple operation to manoeuvre the world's heaviest man-made object at 19,000 tons. Around 200 men worked day and night over several months to construct huge wooden grids and other structures to support the ship as it was beached. A pier of loose stone from the beach was also constructed for visitors to gain a good view of the ship, whose length spanned 692ft.

At the time, the ship owners were recovering from poor press coverage, with Americans slating the quality of the service. Just prior to leaving for Neyland, one excursion from New York to Cape May brought complaints of 'fights on board, struggles for water, scrambles for mattresses, hopeless attempts to gain refreshments, intoxicated stewards, bewildered n****r waiters, fabulous prices of food and drink, disgusting series of rough practical jokes', and so on. Amid mounting debt and a shortage of passengers, *The Pembrokeshire Herald* highlighted problems with the quality of workmanship, reporting, 'The truth is the Company is in a fix'.

Ironically, the ship's presence in Neyland attracted a huge number of tourists, who arrived by train from London, Cheltenham, Gloucester and South Wales. In September 1860, the trains brought more than 2,000 sightseers each day, boosting the local economy with the new demand for hotels, shops, chapels and services.

The *Great Eastern* stayed for six months, but its future was one of continued disappointments before it finally ended up as a showboat in Liverpool. One of its legacies was the naming of a row of cottages that were being built at the time as the Great Eastern Terrace.

The town experienced a boom period over the second half of the nineteenth century. However, a setback occurred in 1906 when the Irish traffic was shifted from Neyland to Goodwick (below Fishguard), where a harbour was built. It suffered a further blow in 1964 when the railway terminus closed.

In 1985, the creation of the Neyland Yacht Haven provided new leisure opportunities and developments since have included eco-friendly lodges which float on recycled pontoons. The annual 'Beating of the Bounds' service, involving a motorboat procession to Haverfordwest, commemorates the traditional rights of fishery.

PEMBROKE

A few years ago, the *Rough Guide to Wales* rather unkindly suggested that 'Pembroke is rather dull', despite its splendid castle, which is the oldest in the county, beginning with an earth-and-wood (motte-and-bailey) variety built by the Norman Baron Roger de Montgomery around 1093.

William Marshal, regarded as the greatest of medieval knights, directed the building of the first stone castle in 1201, which included a huge keep. Marshal was credited with bringing peace to the county and served five English kings: Henry II, his sons, the 'Young King' Henry, Richard I, John, and finally, John's son, Henry III. In 2022, a splendid statue of Marshal on horseback was unveiled outside the castle. This is not without controversy in an age when historical monuments of 'the great and the good' are under close scrutiny, given Marshal's role in the conquest of Wales.

The most famous figure associated with Pembroke Castle is Henry Tudor, who was born here in 1457 when the castle was in the hands of Jasper Tudor, his uncle. Archaeologists digging in the grounds during 2018 discovered the remains of a major mansion or hall which they now think was where Henry Tudor was born. It is significant in castle architecture because it was always thought that the castle grounds were occupied by smaller timber structures rather than high-status residential buildings.

One of the distinctive points about the castle was that it was never captured by the Welsh, unlike other Norman castles of the time. It remained a Parliamentarian stronghold during the Civil Wars, initially supported by the Mayor of Pembroke, John Poyer.

However, when he changed allegiances to support Charles I, this called for Oliver Cromwell himself to lay siege to the castle to reclaim it for the Parliamentarians. Cromwell used gunpowder to destroy many of the castle's features and secure its surrender.

Its present appearance owes much to the restoration work carried out from the nineteenth century onwards. In the 1830s, Thomas Roscoe regarded the castle as 'the most extensive and magnificent' in Wales and he suggested to fellow visitors that the best approach was by water from 'Pennar Mouth'.

Main Street runs the length of the town and contains two historic Anglican churches, nonconformist chapels, a range of Georgian houses, boutiques and gift shops. In 1972, Pembroke was designated a Conservation Area in recognition of its national historic importance and architectural merit.

The castle continues to be central to the fortunes of the town, drawing in tourists and acting as a venue for local events. In 2021, Pembrokeshire County Council received £4.1 million from the UK Government's Levelling Up Fund and has plans to use part of the funding to develop a new Henry Tudor Centre, community hub, library and café alongside the castle.

PEMBROKE DOCK

Modern-day Pembroke Dock grew out of a small medieval village called Paterchurch. A fourteenth-century manor house tower is all that survives within the walls of the dockyard, which was built in 1814. This Royal Naval Dockyard was unique in Wales, created solely as a shipbuilding facility.

Understandably, the town's history has been viewed very much through the lens of the dockyard, which was arguably one of the most important in global maritime history. Phil Carradice maintains, in his history of the town, that the warships built here were the envy of the world, being so revolutionary that they changed the course of naval history. During the dockyard's history, five royal yachts and 262 other royal vessels were built.

Early visitors were most impressed by the dockyard. In 1836, the travel writer Thomas Roscoe was taken aback by 'the orderly and efficient manner in which these public works are conducted'. He conveyed the bustle of the dockyard, on one side huge blocks of oak which form the largest ships, on the other immense anchors destined to become the hopes of thousands of mariners in their hour of peril. As one ship was ready to leave the stocks, the skeleton of another was taking shape. Roscoe took great pride in the efforts he saw at first hand to maintain 'national glory and importance'.

The strategic value of the dockyard called for the protective presence of a garrison of Royal Marines. They were accommodated in purpose-built barracks in 1846, which were expanded considerably in the building of the red-brick Llanion Barracks, completed in 1906. These could cater for up to seventy officers and 2,000 other ranks. The site also included stables, gun sheds, canteen, hospital and parade ground.

The military presence in the town created a demand for services, including pubs and prostitutes. Phil Carradice points out that the Rising Sun, which stood at the bottom of Brewery Street, was well known as a 'waiting room' where soldiers queued before entering a nearby brothel. This was finally closed in 1913 following a police raid.

Not every pub in the town was a den of debauchery. The Victoria Inn, for example, was a well-run tavern which had its own ballroom.

Other services developed to meet the needs of an expanding population. The first major elementary schools opened in 1845, supported by the Admiralty and dockyard officers as well as the Church. This National School soon established a good reputation.

The town also hosted one of the three markets in the county (along with Tenby and Fishguard). The building was once used by Wild Bill Hickock to stable his horses and equipment during his show in the early 1900s. An early vending machine which dispensed postcards and penny postage stamps, complete with paper and envelopes, can be seen on the wall outside the market.

In August 1902, King Edward VII briefly toured the yards and visited nearby Monkton Priory. The dockyard was building the large steel cruisers which would later fight in the Battle of Jutland during the First World War.

In wartime, more than 4,000 people worked in the dockyard, and in the 1930s, the Royal Air Force used the site as a base for its flying boats, including the Sunderland in 1938, which continued in service until the late 1950s. Arthur Harris was the commanding officer at the base in 1933. He was later to mastermind the British bombing campaigns in Germany during the Second World War, earning the nickname 'Bomber Harris', when he took charge of Bomber Command.

In more recent times, the former dockyard has become a commercial port and, along with Fishguard, a main ferry service to Ireland. The dockyard is also a conservation area and landscape of historic interest, featuring numerous former naval monuments, ponds, slips and buildings.

In 2021, much to the angst of conservation societies, the Milford Haven Port Authority (MHPA) submitted plans to the local authority to infill many of the quays and historic shipbuilding areas. To mitigate changes, the MHPA set out several measures, including renovating historic buildings such as the Sunderland Hangar Annexes, reusing stonework and adding interpretation tools. The £60m project, funded by a combination of government and private investment, aims to support post-Covid economic recovery and update the maritime facilities, for example by adding fabrication and launch facilities.

The Pembroke Dock Heritage Centre tells the story of the town's unique connections with the navy, army and air force. It operates from the Royal Dockyard Chapel, the only surviving Georgian military chapel in Wales.

SAUNDERSFOOT

At the start of the nineteenth century, Saundersfoot was little more than a hamlet of half a dozen or so houses and a couple of inns. Its development is tied to coal, with indications that coal was being mined in the area as early as the 1320s. Villagers worked mainly in transporting coal and culm down to the beach, where it was loaded onto small boats and, in some cases, shipped to France and Ireland.

In 1829, the building of an enlarged, new harbour and railway linked to new collieries in Begelly and Kilgetty represented major investments. Further expansion followed when Charles Ranken Vickerman, a businessman from Essex, established a new ironworks at Stepaside. Such development was justified, given that in the boom years of the 1880s, an annual coal production reached 100,000 tons.

The village prospered until the Bonville Court Colliery closed in the 1930s. Since then, tourism has taken over as the main industry, with visitors attracted to the fine, sandy beaches.

The changes in the village are recorded by historian Roscoe Howells, born in Saundersfoot. His evocative history includes images of miners queueing up to collect their pay and loading coal in the harbour, old clom cottages heated by culm, beer being delivered to pubs by horse and cart along the sands, and a picture of 93-year-old Martha Richards taken in 1974, the last woman to have worked in the Stepaside Pits.

ST DAVIDS

Historically, St Davids is regarded as the holiest of Welsh places (Figure 25). In the 1930s H.V. Morton called it 'the church with the longest memory in Britain', while the author Jan Morris describes St Davids as where one feels 'the hush that is the unmistakable pause of holiness'.

St Davids was of significance even before David settled here in the sixth century. Neolithic burial chambers have been found nearby on St Davids Head at Coetan Arthur and on Carn Llidi.

Given the resources and stamina needed to go on pilgrimage to the Holy Land or Rome, St Davids (then known as Menevia) offered an attractive alternative, inspired by the saying that there was as much merit in going to St Davids twice as there was in going once to Rome. There was also a superstition that every man must go to St Davids once, either dead or alive.

In 1123, Pope Calixtus II granted the privilege of pilgrimage to St Davids, which affirmed an ancient practice. One story suggested that it was so popular that over time the tiles had worn parts or grooves showing where pilgrims knelt to pray. In 1171, Henry II visited St Davids, where he offered two choral caps of velvet for the singers in serving God and St David, together with a handful of silver, about 10 shillings. The amount of money donated to the chapels was said to be so much that it was measured out in dishes rather than counted.

It is hard to imagine what pilgrims thought as they reached the climax of their journey, but they could be forgiven for thinking this was at the end of the world. The travel writer Peter Sager describes the peninsula as 'a Welsh Land's End'. In fact, the windswept *Dewisland* was strategically well placed, with close links to Ireland and, via the seaways, relatively safe passage to Scotland, north-west England and Cornwall, and thence Brittany and the Continent.

The modern visitor might think that this was an ideal spot to get away from it all, but St Davids was centre stage in the development of the Christian Church and the politics that came with it. Traditionally, bishops were freely elected and so when, in 1114, Henry I forced the appointment of his own man, the Norman Bishop Barnard, it was seen as a major slight against the clergy of Wales. However, the Normans were keen to promote the cult of St David because this was seen as a way of unifying the western part of their territories.

Fig. 25 St Davids Cathedral. (*Fenton, 1811, opposite p.71*)

The diocese was a large one, covering 80 miles north and east, stretching to the Herefordshire border. Under Norman administration, the Bishop of St Davids was a Marcher lord, which meant that he had significant power and wealth. Bishop Sulien, who hosted the visit of William the Conqueror, earned a reputation as 'the best and wisest man in all of Wales'. He oversaw the work and welfare of the clergy within the diocese.

Bishops are often depicted as holding two keys: one to open the door into a person's soul and the other to unlock the gates of the Kingdom of Heaven. The bishop had a special chair within the church known as a cathedra, which is why the church of St Davids is also called a cathedral. The surviving cathedra measures almost 29ft in height.

Legend has it that David struck the ground with his staff during a dry summer and a spring bubbled forth. The spring still exists, although a well was later built over it, concealed beneath the ground outside the Lady Chapel. Much of the existing building dates from the late twelfth century onwards. It is difficult to trace the exact sequence of building work, with reports of a collapsing tower in 1220 and an earthquake in 1247 causing considerable destruction. The builders faced enduring problems, which included sloping floors and waterlogged ground.

Bishop Henry de Gower (1328–47) is regarded as the greatest of the medieval bishops of St Davids. He supervised major changes to the cathedral, including the building of his own tomb. The present Bishop's Palace is essentially his work and once boasted private suites, major and minor halls for ceremonies, and a wide range of service rooms. It is regarded as the 'apogee of the medieval magnate's house'. De Gower also refurbished the palace at Lamphey by adding accommodation.

In its heyday, in around 1400, the bishopric included the cathedral and palace at St Davids and three other palaces at Llawhaden, Lamphey and Abergwili. St Davids Palace was an impressive building with the bishop having a private room ('solar'), hall and chapel, a great hall for special occasions, barrel vaults for storage under the main building, guest rooms, state-of-the-art kitchen and fishpond. It was a working community.

By the 1500s, St Davids was the largest church in Wales, spanning 92m, and included the finely carved oak nave ceiling. As part of the Dissolution of the Monasteries, lead was stripped from the roof and Bishop William Barlow sold the metal to provide his five daughters with dowries large enough so that they could all marry bishops.

The northern side of the cathedral tower is the only one without a clockface, because the parishioners in the north could not afford to raise enough money for one to be installed facing them. The decline in pilgrimages following the Reformation affected St Davids to the extent that by the 1800s it was in 'a state of unfeeling desertion'.

In 2010, a pilgrimage was organised to raise funds to restore a medieval shrine to St David, which had been damaged during the Reformation.

The costs of maintaining the cathedral are around £2,700 a day. In 1932, Watkyn Morgan, then dean, created the Friends of St Davids Cathedral, which continues to raise funds. The contributions of visitors and pilgrims are key to maintaining the cathedral, although not everyone appreciates the crowds. In 1936, the artist Cedric Morris found it 'a madly depressing experience – the Cathedral sitting like an outraged hen in the middle of a howling mob'. Prior to the pandemic outbreak, the cathedral typically attracted around 270,000 visitors each year.

One of the most significant events in modern times was the appointment in 2016 of Joanna Penberthy as the 129th Bishop of St Davids, following a succession of 128 men to the role. She was consecrated in January 2017, becoming the first female bishop in the Church in Wales. Her political views led to controversy when in 2021 she tweeted 'never, never trust a Tory', which led to a public apology and something of an embarrassment to the Church, given the historic ties between the Conservatives and Anglicans.

Artists are drawn to the landscape and light quality of the St Davids peninsula. The town has numerous art and craft galleries.

TENBY

The origins and growth of Tenby are associated with the fishing industry. The town's Welsh name, *Dinbych-y-pysgod* means 'Little fortress of the fish'. It became one of the main herring ports of South Wales. The town was first mentioned in a ninth-century poem 'In praise of Tenby', describing the town as 'a fine fortress of revel and tumult', a tag that has stood the test of time. By the twelfth century it was considered important enough for the Normans to build a castle on the headland and, later, stout 20ft town walls to keep out Welsh attacks.

When John Leland visited Tenby about 1540, he found very wealthy merchants living in a town that was 'strongeli waullid and welle gatid, everi gate having his portcolis'. In 1588, under Elizabeth I, the fortifications were strengthened out of fear that Tenby may be attacked by the Spanish. The Five Arches is the most famous gateway and carries a plaque, '1588, E.R.'

The building of St Mary's Church was a sign of Tenby's medieval wealth, but the town soon entered a long period of economic decline. Key trade with Spain and France suffered as relations with Britain deteriorated. Further disruption followed the Civil Wars, when in 1643 Cromwell laid siege to the Royalist town for three days. It fell again to Cromwell's forces in 1648 and following the Plague of 1651 the town suffered further setback with estimates of 1,000 deaths, one in three of the town's population. Pigs were running through uninhabited streets.

Tenby's economy took time to recover. The artist Charles Norris described it in 1826 as a 'poor neglected fishing town – totally unknown to the luxurious and deserted by the enterprising'.

This was an overstatement. Already by the 1780s there were signs of improvement. The town council widened streets to accommodate increasing traffic, repaired parapets for walking and approved lodging houses for commercial travellers.

The late eighteenth century saw an influx of tourists into Wales as the Napoleonic Wars restricted Continental travel and the mail coach to Tenby eased access. New Georgian hotels, houses, inns and restaurants started to appear. Lexden Terrace, overlooking St Catherine's Island and Castle Beach, has the finest row of Georgian houses in Wales. Tenby was a town on the rise.

The enduring attraction of Tenby's sea bathing, with its clear and clean waters, was key to its economic recovery and development as a seaside resort. Tenby offered sweeping beaches, romantic cliffs, the mystery of Caldey Island and pure air, free from 'unwholesome smoke' and the noise and bustle of the busier commercial towns in South Wales. The wonderfully named *Cambrian Traveller's Guide in Every Direction*, published in 1813, described Tenby as 'unequalled for the beauty of its bay and convenience of sea bathing'.

In 1810, a new bathhouse opened in the present Laston House, with hot and cold facilities, public and private baths, dressing rooms, tearoom and kitchen. Over the entrance ran a quote from Euripides: 'All man's pollution does the sea cleanse.' The message was clear enough: swimming and bathing were good for you as they stimulated and invigorated the body.

But this came at a price. Warm baths were 2*s* 6*d* per person and hot showers 1*s* 6*d*, though one could swim for 9*d*. Such prices meant that locals wanting a swim were left to find remote spots at the ends of beaches away from the gaze of visitors. One naturalist was pleased to see 'female peasantry enjoying without disguise the delicious coolness and delight of bathing in the open sea'.

Sea bathing was quite a cosmetic and ritualistic affair. As Ruth Goodman points out, it meant little more than standing in waist-deep water and dunking oneself two or three times under the surface, climbing out, drying off and changing back into normal daywear.

Fig. 26 Tenby, *c*.1837. (*Roscoe, 1837, opposite p.141*)

For women, it was quite an ordeal to get changed into a bathing suit. For modesty, the swimwear had to be long to cover much of the body (Figure 27). While the woollen material provided some warmth, it was also heavy and cumbersome. Any movement, let alone swimming, was difficult and so women typically spent no more than ten or so minutes paddling in the water.

Moreover, vigorous activity in the sea was not considered ladylike behaviour. On the other hand, men sometimes swam naked. Sarah Wilmot, writing in her journal of 1795, was appalled at the thought of naked bathing in Tenby – 'a disgrace of common decency'. However, a Tenby by-law of 1842 ruled:

Bathing Dresses.

Fig. 27 Bathing dresses.
(*South Wales Daily News*,
8 August 1899)

> No person shall bathe, between the hours of eight in the morning and nine in the evening, except from a bathing machine, or shall be naked on any part of the South Sands … the North Sands … or in the sea from any boat within two hundred yards of the sands or shore.

Bathing machines, which were like beach huts on wheels, were available to provide privacy while dressing. In 1843, the charges were 9*d* for each person, 4*d* for each child, and 6*d* per head within a family. When Philip Gosse visited the beaches in 1854, he was taken aback by the 'uncouth, uncorsetted figures' wearing blue serge gowns, who directed affairs.

An earlier generation of these bathing women included the likes of Peggy Davies. She worked for forty-two years tending to ladies who visited the town. On 29 September 1809, while in the water herself, she 'was seized with apoplexy and expired'. She was 82 years old. Funds were raised to commemorate her service with a tablet in St Mary's Church, which acknowledged her 'good humour, respectful attention, and gratitude' [which] made her employers friends'.

Advertisers saw the potential of bathing machines, much to the irritation of one observer. 'To see a bathing van at Tenby is to be annoyingly informed, in large letters, that "Beecham's pills are worth a guinea a box".'

In the early nineteenth century, a healthy break by the seaside was a luxury that the working classes could not afford. It was the railway, combined with the Bank Holidays Act (1871), which put seaside holidays initially within the reach of the middle classes and, as ticket prices fell by the end of the century, working-class families.

A strict dress code remained in place through to the 1900s, as photographs of Edwardian Tenby and other Pembrokeshire seaside towns reveal. Interestingly, naturism (naked bathing) took off, so to speak, in the interwar period as more liberal post-war attitudes developed.

Tenby's appeal went beyond the health benefits of being beside the sea. The vicinity also attracted the academically minded, particularly in the natural sciences as interest in Charles Darwin's theory of evolution developed. In 1855, Thomas Henry Huxley (who later coined the term 'agnosticism') studied local barnacles on Tenby's beaches to correct a minor error in a paper by Darwin that he had recently reviewed.

He was on honeymoon with his seriously ill wife, Henrietta Heathorn, with whom he waited on and carried daily to the seaside. She acted as his scientific assistant, making sketches and descriptions of the fauna he dissected. Later in life, she reminisced, 'The whole atmosphere was scientific. Little by little I understood the great problems that underlay the dissection of even a fish or plant [...] of the interchange of force and heat, of the wonders of chemical changes.'

This appetite for advancing knowledge was reflected by archaeologists and antiquarians, geologists, biologists and naturalists. Bradshaw's famous *Descriptive Railway Handbook of Great Britain and Ireland*, published in 1863, noted that half of Britain's 600 varieties of seashell had been found on the Tenby coastline.

During the 1860s, the idea of forming a museum was mooted for 'the interest and instruction of residents and visitors'. But it was not until 1878 that Tenby Museum formally opened, with its collections of shells, insects and plants, scientific books and articles of interest. It stands as the oldest independent museum in Wales and was later renamed as the Tenby Museum and Art Gallery.

As Tenby's fortunes revived in the nineteenth and early twentieth centuries, people had more disposable income. They could spend this on a range of entertainment and sports offered through musical promenades, fancy dress and evening balls, theatre performances, billiards, cricket, lawn tennis, sailing and races on the south sands, while markets were held on Wednesdays and Saturdays.

Golf appealed to the middle classes. Tenby Golf Club, established in 1888, is the oldest in Wales. The rugby club was formed in 1901.

And those seeking to refurbish their homes in the latest styles could turn to a new departmental store which opened in 1902. T.P. Hughes had trained in a large London departmental store and wanted to bring fresh ideas back to his native town.

The town's increasing wealth meant that the infrastructure and public services could develop. In 1896, the *Tenby Observer* announced that 'a new epoch in the educational history of Tenby' had begun with the opening of its intermediate school at Greenhill. It was intermediate in the sense of operating between primary and further education. These schools were designed to offer a technical education so that middle-class children, who could not afford the fees of public schools, could become surveyors, clerks and engineers.

In his history of the school, ex-headmaster Wilfred Harrison noted that most of the early admissions were the children of tradesmen – tobacconists, hairdressers, jewellers, booksellers, bakers, ironmongers and the like. In practice, few of the intermediate schools in Wales quite lived up to their intention (Pembroke Dock, with its proximity to the dockyard, was an exception), but they did provide a broad-based education which benefited many, including a pool of prospective teachers.

In 1897 Tenby Pier was extended and reopened in 1899 by the Duchess of York. Officially named the Royal Victoria Pier, it was a calling place for steamers from other piers and resorts in South Wales, north Devon and Somerset. During the summer, band concerts were given on the pier-head and the pier became a very popular angling centre. It was demolished between 1946 and 1953, having fallen into disrepair during the Second World War.

In the 1950s and 1960s working-class miners' families from the valleys boarded coaches for a day's outing while the middle classes from the Midlands and South Wales with money to spend booked into bed and breakfast or hotel accommodation for the school holidays. Roger Lockley's first edition of *Pembrokeshire*, which appeared in 1957, welcomed 'day-visitors from the smoke-grimed narrow valleys' for whom 'Tenby must seem like a glimpse of heaven'.

Tenby was also a popular destination for Sunday school trips. The *Ward Tourist Guide* from the 1960s summed up the town's appeal, 'The picturesque seafront, the splendid sands, the marvellous colour of the water, the wealth of the sunshine and the freshness of the air'.

The development of low-cost air travel in the 1970s and the rise of the Spanish tourist resorts meant that Tenby had to adapt to remain competitive. The hotels did so by increasingly catering for older visitors and coach tours, while caravan sites and chalet developments around Tenby offered cheap self-catering breaks. Kiln Park and Lydstep Haven led the way.

A few years ago, the *Rough Guide to Wales* described Tenby as 'everything a seaside resort should be'. It retains the natural and historic strengths of sweeping beaches, boat trips, clifftop walks, quaint shops, stunning views and ice cream parlours. While it may have lost something of its genteel past and the Victorian hotels along the Esplanade are not what they were in their heyday, Tenby still has much to offer. It has first-class bathing and views across the bay, the Pembrokeshire Coastal Path winds east to Amroth, while to St Bride's in the west there is another 100 or so miles of clifftop walks and rocky coves. And for those who enjoy a challenge, Tenby hosts the annual Ironman Wales, combining swimming, running and cycling.

20

PEMBROKESHIRE VILLAGES

One of the attractions of Pembrokeshire is visiting its villages, which vary in character, history and topography. The following selection is not exhaustive but indicates such diversity. Geoffrey Davies provides a more detailed commentary in his book on Pembrokeshire villages.

ABEREIDDY

The village is located 5 miles from St Davids. In 2005, the small beach was awarded Blue Flag status. In the nineteenth century, Abereiddy Quarry was among the villages supplying roof slates to the industrial towns of England and Wales. In 1904, the quarry closed and was later dynamited for safety reasons, allowing sea-water to enter and combine with minerals and producing a strong shade of blue. The Blue Lagoon is now a popular diving site.

Several stories are associated with the abandonment of the village. One suggests that a storm destroyed the quarrymen's cottages, while a more fanciful tale relates that an itinerant grocer, visiting on his horse-drawn cart, unwittingly carried typhoid into the village.

AMROTH

Amroth is famous for its long, sandy beach, where it is possible to view the remains of an ancient, petrified forest during extreme low tide. Named after a mound ('*rath*'), it was an important landing place for pilgrims heading to and returning from St Davids (Figure 28). They could take a boat to Cardiff or across to Bristol, thus avoiding the discomfort of muddy roads and the danger of being robbed.

The much-admired smokeless coal from the parish was shipped from Wiseman's Bridge to Bristol. John Colby, a local mine owner, built Colby Lodge in 1803, which is now under the care of the National Trust.

The mansion at Amroth Castle dates to around 1800, with only a much-restored gate surviving from earlier times. Sir Owen Cosby-Philipps, a successful businessman and Member of Parliament, owned the castle but in 1931 was imprisoned for falsifying financial company records. The castle became a holiday venue, reflecting the local economy's transition from mining to tourism.

ANGLE

Angle has a rich history, with Neolithic origins and numerous listed buildings of significance, including an almshouse, former National School, medieval Tower House, Chapel Bay Fort and cottages, St Mary's Church and the fifteenth-century Sailors' Chapel located within its churchyard. The chapel, restored in the nineteenth century, was founded by Edward de Shirburn, 'knight of Nangle'. The drowned bodies of sailors were taken here. The churchyard also includes a Preaching Cross, which marked the spot for outdoor preaching.

Fig. 28 Seafaring pilgrims. (*Thornhill-Timmins, 1895, p.131*)

The early eighteenth-century Point House Inn was a meeting place for pirates and smugglers. According to legend, if the fire inside the pub was ever extinguished then bad luck would follow. The pub closed in 2020.

The nineteenth-century Rocket Cart House is significant in the history of the Coastguard Service. It was in use until the 1930s as the base for a cliff rescue team who deployed rockets, lines and buoys.

BOSHERSTON

This village is said to be named after Bosher, one of the followers of the de Stackpole family who arrived with William the Conqueror. The Bosher name was still known in the 1930s when Mary Jones, the local schoolteacher, wrote her village history, now available in digital format on the National Library of Wales website. Jones mentioned the delights of hearing the locals converse using words derived from a mix of Flemish, Danish, Saxon, Norman and Irish influence. For example, '*stivle*' meant 'very cold', '*mixen*' referred to a 'heap of manure' and '*scaldy pluck*' described children racing for sweets.

Bosherston is also famous for its water lily ponds. They were created in the late eighteenth century by blocking three streams. Legend says that it was here that King Arthur yielded up Excalibur to the Lady of the Lake, although this is a common claim among various other sites.

CAREW

Carew is dominated by its magnificent castle, which was the work of Sir Nicholas de Carew, who fought for Edward I in the wars against the Welsh. Archaeologists have found evidence of occupation on the site dating back to the Iron Age. The most famous occupant was Sir Rhys ap Thomas, who held an extravagant tournament in 1507 to celebrate his appointment to the Order of the Garter. This was the most senior order of knighthood. Sir Rhys (Figure 29) proved a key figure in the rise of *Harri Tudur*, the future King Henry VII.

In the 1580s, Sir John Perrot ordered major changes to the castle fabric, including adding the magnificent north range, widely regarded as an Elizabethan masterpiece. Perrot's library boasted works of French, Spanish, Greek and Latin and the house held the sixteenth-century equivalent of a modern sound studio with instruments such as cornets, an Irish harp, flute and recorders; bedrooms of beautiful walnut beds with canopies of hanging silk, velvet or taffeta, fringed with lace or gold; new innovations such as cupboards; floors covered with lavish Turkish carpets and Irish rugs, while Damask cushions and sarcenet quilts adorned different rooms. In short, this was a showpiece home, a statement of contemporary, international fashion.

The Carew Cross is a memorial to Maredudd, who ruled the region between 1033–35. Its Celtic design inspired the logo for Cadw, the government body responsible for the preservation of Welsh monuments ('*cadw*' is the Welsh word meaning 'to protect' or 'keep').

In the nineteenth century, tenant farmers were paid to quarry limestone in the parish. They used hand tools and explosives that were transported in by cart from Saundersfoot and Pembroke Dock. The limestone was shipped to the lime kilns along the Pembrokeshire and Cardiganshire coast. Successive generations of the Scourfield family have quarried limestone and continue to produce limestone aggregate products at Carew Quarries.

Fig. 29 Nineteenth-century painting of Sir Rhys ap Thomas, showing Carew Castle in the background. (*National Library of Wales*)

CILGERRAN

Cilgerran has a picturesque castle which was built in the early 1100s by the Norman Gerald de Windsor, grandfather of Giraldus Cambrensis. In 1109, the castle was attacked by the Welshman Owain ap Cadwgan, and it is said de Windsor only managed to escape by sliding down the privy. Owain then seduced Gerald's wife, Nest.

It was 100 years later before the Anglo-Normans recaptured the castle under the direction of the imposing William Marshal. The castle subsequently changed hands several times. After Owain Glyndwr's siege in the early fifteenth century, little is heard about Cilgerran. As a romantic ruin, however, it caught the interest of artists such as Richard Wilson and J.M.W. Turner.

CRYMYCH

This large village developed with the arrival of the railway in 1874 and passenger services the following year. The station, located on the Whitland to Cardigan line, was named after the Crymych Arms, a nearby pub which was the only building in the area. In 1886, the railway line was extended 27½ miles to Cardigan and was known as the 'Cardi Bach'. It closed in the 1960s, along with many other branch lines. The local Welsh-medium newspaper, *Y Cardi Bach*, has been running since 1979. In recent years, part of the disused railway line has been transformed into a cycle path.

As Crymych was at the intersection of six roads, it was a popular meeting place for drovers before driving their cattle in different directions. They could have headed north-east through Newcastle Emlyn and on to mid-Wales and the Midlands, or taken the south-east route through Carmarthen and on to London and south England.

General stores, banks and places of worship continued to serve the agricultural community after the closure of the railway in the 1960s. The secondary school, Ysgol Y Preseli, opened in 1958. Before then, pupils in the north of the county who passed the eleven-plus examination attended school either in Narberth or Cardigan. In 2022, the all-through Welsh-medium Ysgol Bro Preseli (3–19) replaced the village primary and secondary school.

Within a couple of miles of Crymych is the mountain of Frenni Fawr. This is also known as Macsen's Fort, named after Magnus Maximus or Macsen, the Roman commander who became Emperor of the West. It is also linked to stories of the Tylwyth Teg, or fairies, who offered a local shepherd boy all the delights he could imagine, provided he did not drink from a local well where the golden fish swam. As with Eve in the Garden of Eden, he fell to temptation. As he drank, his riches disappeared, and he stood alone shivering on the cold mountain top.

DALE

Dale is most famous for being the place where Henry Tudor landed in 1485 with his fifty-five ships and 4,000 men on his way to Bosworth Field. As Morton put it, 'The world said goodbye to the Middle Ages when Henry Tudor stepped ashore at Milford Haven.' In 1985, the villagers marked the 500th anniversary in lavish style.

Dale is also famous for the *Sea Empress* oil spillage in 1996, when 72,000 tons of crude oil poured into the sea with devastating impact. Estimates vary, but up to 15,000 birds may have been killed. Around 200km of coastline was covered in crude oil. The cost of the clean-up was around £60 million. The *Sea Empress* was a single-hulled tanker; nowadays, most are double hulls, which significantly reduces the likelihood of oil spillage.

The village is a popular attraction for windsurfing, sailing and other watersports. Visits to Skomer and the other islands are also a major attraction, booked through Pembrokeshire Islands Boat Trips which has operated for more than forty years.

EGLWYSWRW

Eglwyswrw is named after St Eirw, who was said to be buried in the church in Elizabethan times. The church was completely rebuilt in 1829 on the site of a much older church and dedicated to Cristiolus, a sixth-century Welsh saint. The seventeenth-century

Sergeant's Inn is a grade-II-listed building which once held the county court sessions but has also served as a chapel and school.

Historically, the village is proud of its Welsh language and culture. However, in 2022, the community council voiced concerns over the impact on the Welsh language of a new housing scheme. Around 60 per cent of those within the Crymych ward speak Welsh, which is significantly higher than the Pembrokeshire and national average of around 19 per cent.

LLANGWM

Llangwm has long been considered a Flemish settlement but tangible evidence for this has been thin on the ground. In 2016, a Heritage Lottery-funded project ('The Search for Little Flanders') set out to explore the village origins using DNA, placename evidence, archaeological excavations at the medieval manor house and interviews with historians and archivists. One of the most interesting findings was the genetic match between a local resident and the de la Roche family, who were prominent Flemish landowners in the 1100s, as well as modern-day relatives living in Flanders.

The 'Talking Tapestry' exhibited at St Jerome's Church tells the story of 'Llangum', one of the earlier names of the village. The village was once described by the *Tenby Observer* as comprising 'clean, thrifty, sober people'.

The fisherwomen of Llangwm have long attracted attention, famed for their hardiness in walking many miles to market their catches. (Figure 30). The women had a tough, puritanical reputation and were said to oppose danc-

Fig. 30 Llangwm fisherwomen.
(*Thornhill-Timmins, 1895, p.181*)

ing and the influence of outsiders. Thornhill-Timmins observed in 1895 that girls had only recently been allowed out of the village as domestic servants.

This was a close-knit, protective community. In 1900, the Llangwm Riots took place, when a hostile crowd led by women took issue with John Morris Philpin, who evicted his widowed sister, Jane Palmer, from a tenement at the rear of his house. Windows were smashed and constables assaulted, but the case was dropped due to lack of evidence.

The thriving local history society hosts exhibitions and talks on wide-ranging subjects. The village also holds an annual literary festival, although this was interrupted with the outbreak of Covid-19.

MAENCLOCHOG

Maenclochog owes its name to its topographic features: the Irish word '*clochog*' means 'craggy place' and '*maen*' is the Welsh word for 'stone'. One myth, suggested in a nineteenth-century gazetteer, was that the name derived from a large stone or cromlech, which was destroyed by villagers seeking hidden treasure.

The village had its own railway station which opened in 1876 along the Narberth Road and Maenclochog Railway line. This was built to serve several small slate quarries in the Preseli Hills.

In October 1943, the English engineer Barnes Wallis visited the area to conduct secret bombing trials following the success of his bouncing bombs during the famous Dambusters Raid in May. Wallis arranged for smaller versions to be dropped on the Maenclochog Railway tunnel (opened in 1876) that had been commissioned for the war effort. The plan was to use these bombs to destroy German railway supply routes to the front, ahead of the D-Day landings in June 1944.

The tunnel was extensively damaged and service personnel were directed to collect all fragments. However, some of these were overlooked, hidden in marshy, inaccessible ground nearby only to be discovered fifty years later. The Yorkshire Air Museum, which hosts the Barnes Wallis Collection, includes one of the large bomb fragments. Despite the success of the trial, Wallis designed and effectively deployed another bomb ('Tallboy'), which had the advantage of burying itself into the ground before exploding.

MANORBIER

Manorbier's name derives from the manor of Pyr, who was the Prior of Caldey Island.

There is evidence of hunter-gatherer activity in the area dating back 12,000 years ago, with the discovery of flint arrowheads and tools. In the Iron Age, two coastal forts were built, the earthworks of which survive.

The first written evidence for Manorbier comes from Gerald de Barri, better known as Giraldus Cambrensis, or Gerald of Wales. He was born in the castle that his ancestors built in the early 1100s (Figure 31). In 1188, during his recruitment tour for the Crusades, Gerald described with fondness the castle fishpond, orchard, hazelnut trees and watermill, concluding that this was 'a spot without equal', even though he didn't visit the castle while on tour.

The fishpond was both a status symbol to contemporaries and a

Fig. 31 Manorbier Castle. (*Roscoe, 1837, opposite p.148*)

source of income. Carp were introduced from Flanders, offering fishermen something different to trout and salmon. The castle also had a 70-acre park stocked with deer, cattle and horses.

In the fourteenth century, a remarkable woman called Alice Perrers bought the Manorbier estate from the de Barri family. Perrers caught the eye of Edward III when she was lady-in-waiting to his wife, Queen Philippa. Legend has it that on his deathbed she took his ring and anything else that was portable. She owned lots of property, although there's no evidence that she visited Manorbier.

Manorbier retained its close-knit community over the centuries. According to a Hearth Tax of 1670, there were only ninety-two dwellings in the whole parish. In 1813, *The Cambrian* listed Manorbier as 'consisting of a few inhabited cottages and a great number in ruins'. The population in 1841 was only 103, although a school did open in 1873.

The village has attracted many creative thinkers, including the artists John Piper and Augustus and Gwen John, the writer Virginia Wolf, the war poet Siegfried Sassoon, the playwright George Bernard Shaw and the novelist Leslie Kenton. In the 1940s and 1950s Francis Byng-Stamper (who lived in Manorbier Castle) and her sister Caroline Byng Lucas were influential figures in the art world, sponsoring the likes of Graham Sutherland and Ceri Richards. They used the castle as a retreat to inspire others.

MARLOES

This is the most westerly village in south Pembrokeshire. There are signs of prehistoric settlement, with an Iron Age fort built at the Deer Park.

The villagers made their living from the sea. Laver, or edible seaweed, was gathered from rocks and stones. It was washed in seven changes of water to remove grit and sand, then it was boiled for seven hours, drained and chopped finely into a green-black pulp. Finally, it was tossed in oatmeal and fried in bacon fat, and usually served with bacon. Laverbread, known as 'Welsh caviar', over time found a market through delicatessens and first-class restaurants.

The Pembrokeshire Liberal Association directed the building of the village clock tower in 1904 to honour Lord Kensington, who died in 1896 and whose family was a major local landowner. St Peter's Church includes an immersion pool or baptistry, built to counter the growing local interest in Baptist beliefs (the Moriah Baptist Chapel had opened in 1892).

The rock formations and pools at Marloes Sands beach and Wooltack Bay are popular tourist attractions. In 2022, the beach was voted the fourth cleanest in the UK based on analysis of water quality, cross-referenced against comments by Google reviewers (Pembrokeshire's Barafundle Bay was voted second).

NEVERN

A different kind of tourist attraction can be found in the ancient village of Nevern. Thousands of visitors arrive each year to see the Bleeding Yew tree and the Celtic Cross in the churchyard. The church has a brass plaque to commemorate George Owen of Henllys and the tomb of Tegid, the poet who helped Lady Charlotte Guest translate the *Mabinogi*.

In pre-Christian times, yew trees had special significance. It was credited with supernatural properties and magic wands were made from its branches. The trees were often planted in church-yards because the foliage acted as a deterrent to cattle.

One legend suggests that the Nevern yew tree oozes sap as a reminder of a monk who was about to be hung from the tree for stealing church plate. He said that the yew would bleed to testify to his innocence. Another theory has it that the tree will continue to weep blood until a Welshman occupies Nevern Castle again.

The new graveyard, on the other side of the road, opened in 1930 and, on a personal note, this is where my grandparents and brother are buried.

The castle was originally built in the eleventh century for Cuhelyn, a local Welsh prince, before it was captured by the Normans. In recent years, the castle has been studied carefully by archaeologists, who have found pottery evidence of trade with Bristol and north Devon. Among the rare findings was a twelfth-century decorated padlock key which may have belonged to an aristocratic lady to safeguard her jewellery or clothes. It has been dubbed 'Angharad's key' after the daughter of Rhys ap Gruffydd (Lord Rhys) the powerful ruler of the region.

Nevern was a meeting place for Welsh princes, who enjoyed jousts and fairs. The Nevern Show is held every August by the local Agricultural and Horticultural Society and is a reminder of these medieval gatherings and showcases local craftwork and produce. The competitions are taken seriously; I recall my grandfather spending hours upon hours tending to his garden vegetables ahead of the show.

PENALLY

Evidence of human occupation at nearby Hoyle's Cave stretches back to 10,000 years ago. The nineteenth-century cave explorations found the bones of animals and birds, such as duck, heron, goose, owls and bear, in its deepest recesses. Today, Hoyle's Cave is an important bat roost and hibernation site. Lesser known is Little Hoyle Cave, a few hundred metres away, where the presence of bear teeth throughout suggests that it was an animal's den.

Penally was an important site for the early Christian saints, with St Teilo born here in the sixth century. The village church, dedicated to St Nicholas, dates to the thirteenth century and features intricately carved crosses.

Above the church on the road to Penally Abbey Hotel is the medieval St Daniel's (St Deiniol's) Well, which has the usual association with healing waters. The hotel has been described by *The Telegraph* as 'Pembrokeshire's loveliest bolthole'. The Mayor of Tenby owned the original house, which was built in the 1840s, and duly installed electricity; he was the first householder to do so in the county. Ironically, when Kiln Park opened in the late 1950s, it had no electricity nor running water. These were added in the 1970s. The modern park has restaurants, a heated pool and tennis courts.

The actor Kenneth Griffith is buried in the village churchyard close to his paternal grandparents. Griffith was persuaded by his Tenby headteacher to drop the 's' from his surname because this was an English deviation. Griffith was a controversial and outspoken figure, never shy of making political comment. Tony Curtis describes how he heard Griffith talking as guest speaker at the Greenhill School anniversary dinner. He shared his sympathies with the Irish Republican Army, saying he would not hesitate to carry a suitcase onto an aeroplane if asked.

PORTHGAIN

Porthgain is now a popular destination for tourists but between 1837 and 1926 it was a centre of industrial activity, exporting slate, bricks and stone for road construction. At its peak around 1918, the harbour received twenty ships a day. Photographs of the village from the 1900s show how busy the village could be with a thriving brick works and sailing ships in the harbour. However, despite modifications to accommodate larger ships, the harbour's remote location and lack of rail links meant that business declined, and the harbour closed in 1931.

The pretty cottages which line the road to the harbour were built to accommodate the slate workers. The work of slaters was exclusively undertaken by men, unlike other industries such as coal, copper and agriculture.

It appears that relations between the slate quarry owners and labourers were good. The former offered reasonable pay and holidays, working conditions were less hazardous than in other regions and the dust-related diseases that were common among those working in the mines or sawmills affected few of the slaters. The pace of work was more measured and accidents were less frequent than underground. Men were still working in the slate industry at 70 and 80 years of age.

ROCH

Roch developed around its thirteenth-century castle, which was built by Adam de Rupe on an outcrop of volcanic rock along the *Landsker* border. According to legend, he was told by a local witch that he needed to survive a year without being bitten by an adder or he would die. Hence, the castle was built out of harm's way. But, on the last day of the year, feeling cold, he asked for a basket of firewood to be brought into the castle – and was bitten by a snake hiding in the wood pile.

Lucy Walter, lover of Charles II, was born in Roch Castle. Some claim they later married, making her Queen of England. Their illegitimate son, James, Duke of Monmouth, was executed for high treason in 1685.

ROSEBUSH

The name Rosebush is a corruption of the Welsh name Rhos-y-bwlch, meaning 'the gap on the moor'. In the 1870s, its location attracted the Kent entrepreneur Edward Cropper to invest and develop the area as a spa resort. He bought the local quarries and paid for the construction of a railway to transport the slate to Clunderwen and Fishguard. He erected cottages to house the quarrymen and a two-storey railway hotel built out of corrugated zinc, known as the *Tafarn Sinc*.

The boom was short-lived as demand fell short of expectations and the inferior quality of slate led to the closure of the quarries in 1905. The pub continues, however, as a community venture. And one of the original steam locomotives, *Margaret* (named after Edward Cropper's wife), survives at the Scolton Manor Museum near Haverfordwest.

STEPASIDE

Stepaside is named after a request by Oliver Cromwell's army for the people to 'step aside' as they marched towards Pembroke during the Civil Wars. It became an industrial village. The ironworks opened in 1849 and the remains of the blast furnaces can be seen in Pleasant Valley. There are also old railway tunnels which connected collieries at Stepaside, Kilgetty and Reynalton to Saundersfoot Harbour, where the coal was loaded into ships. The ironworks was not very productive and closed in 1877 although the colliery continued until the 1930s.

ST DOGMAELS

Named after a Celtic monk, St Dogfael, this is a quaint village of narrow, crowded streets close to the Cardiganshire border. It marks the start (or end) point of the Pembrokeshire Coast Path.

The most famous historical building is the Norman abbey, which was occupied by the Benedictines. Gerald of Wales described how he spent a comfortable night here during his tour of Wales in 1188. The abbey was closed as part of the Dissolution of the Monasteries in 1536–37.

The village's nineteenth-century houses feature distinctive pale blue/silver slate from the Teifi Valley. Many of the occupiers earned their living as fishermen. Rare footage filmed in 1922 shows them bringing in salmon in the shallows of the River Teifi, while visitors helped out by rolling up their trousers and skirts![7]

In the north of the village is Albro Castle, a former workhouse which served both Pembrokeshire and Cardiganshire. St Dogmaels is now a popular holiday spot.

ST FLORENCE

Arnulph de Montgomery, the eleventh-century Norman conqueror of Penfro, founded this village. He chose St Florent, who was commemorated in his home district of the Loire Valley, for its name. The oldest part of the village church (west of the nave) dates to the thirteenth century but the outstanding feature is the landmark tower, which was built around 1500.

---

7   The film can be viewed at https://player.bfi.org.uk/free/film/watch-fishing-at-st-dogmaels-1922-online

TAVERNSPITE

Tavernspite originated as a resting place or hospice for medieval pilgrims making their way from Whitland Abbey to St Davids. This is the origin of the village name, a corruption of *Tafarn Ysbyty* ('Tavern of the Hospice'). However, the village only formally received its name in 1721.

Tavernspite was an ideal spot to break a journey, given it was the point where six roads come together. The development of the mail coach route to Ireland meant that, in 1779, the Plume of Feathers opened as an inn to provide accommodation and food, as well as a resting place for the horses.

By the 1840s, the village had five public houses to cater for the increase in traffic. However, their demise over the second half of the nineteenth century followed the opening of a new road through Red Roses to Tenby and the extension of the Great Western Railway to Whitland. In a talk delivered in the village schoolroom in 1891, the Temperance Society successfully lobbied against the opening of another new public house.

WARREN

The village name suggests that rabbits were once bred here, which would not be surprising given the importance of rabbits in the medieval rural economy.

The village church dates from 1290 and has an unusual stone spire. In the 1980s, the church, which had fallen into disrepair, was restored through the voluntary efforts of British and locally stationed German troops. Ironically, it is claimed that the spire was used by Luftwaffe pilots in the Second World War as a navigation landmark on their bombing raids into Pembrokeshire. That aside, the West German Government donated the font cover and altar table, which were made in Germany. The organ, made in 1842, once belonged to the composer Felix Mendelssohn.

21

PEMBROKESHIRE ISLANDS

While there are said to be around 1,000 islands off Pembrokeshire, almost all of these are little more than sea-washed rocks. Of the eight main island groups, three are far out into the Celtic Sea (Grassholm, the Smalls and the Hats and Barrels), while the others are close to the mainland: Caldey and St Margaret's, Skomer and Middleholm, Skokholm, Ramsey, Bishops and Clerks. There are also tidal islands, such as Ynys Meicel, upon which Strumble Head lighthouse is built and Dinas Island, which is technically not an island because it is connected to the mainland by a valley which opens to the sea at both ends.

Historically, people's motive for living on these islands has been to farm, pursue a life of solitude, worship, enjoy or exploit nature. Over the centuries, birds and their eggs have been taken from their nests in vast numbers. For example, puffins were stripped of their feathers which then filled sacks and were shipped off as luxury pillows.

Meanwhile, boys would risk their lives dangling by ropes over cliff edges to collect the eggs of buzzards, peregrines, ravens and guillemots. The television presenter Tony Robinson describes the collection of guillemot eggs as one of the worst jobs in history. It was a practice that dated back to the Vikings, who wintered on islands around Britain while away from home. When food was scarce, they would make ropes from nettles and climb over cliff edges to seize the birds' eggs, but ropes could easily fray, the raiders could lose their footing, or even be attacked by aggressive seabirds (although guillemots are quite docile).

BISHOPS AND CLERKS

These outlying rocks and islets are 1½ miles or so west of Ramsey. One story suggests that they are named after the survivors of a six-teenth-century shipwreck, Miles Bishop, James Clerk and Henry Clerk. Saxton's map of the county, drawn up in 1578, mentions the 'bisshop and his clarkes'. However, this derivation is now thought to be unlikely and the name perhaps comes from there being a larger island surrounded by smaller islands.

The lighthouse of South Bishop was built in 1839 and marks the southernmost tip of the group. This island is owned by Trinity House, whereas the others belong to the Royal Society for the Protection of Birds (RSPB).

CALDEY

The Norse name for Caldey is 'land of the Spring' (*kelda/ey*), which suggests that the Vikings may have used the island as a source of fresh water. Another suggestion is that it means 'Cold Island' (*kaldr/ ey*), with the sense of being uninhabited, vacant or unattractive.

The island's parish church of St David stands on a prehistoric burial ground dating back 2,000 years. Archaeologists think that ancient Celtic burials were in keeping with the belief that islands represented a bridge to the afterlife.

Monks first settled on the island in the sixth century. The first abbot was Pyro, after which the island took its Celtic name *Ynys Pyro* ('Isle of Pyro'), or in Welsh, *Ynys Bŷr*. Unfortunately, Pyro met a premature end when he overindulged in wine and fell into a well or pond.

Caldey has a statue of Samson, the second abbot and teetotal patron saint of the island, who favoured communal monastic life rather than living as a hermit. St Illtyd's Church houses the medieval Ogham Stone, one of the most significant pre-Norman monuments in Wales.

Caldey first entered documented history in 1113 when Henry I granted the island to Robert Fitzmartin, who subsequently ordered the building of an abbey. Within a few years, it was given

Fig. 32 Caldey Abbey, 1907. (*Shepherd, 1907*)

to the Benedictines, who lived in the priory which remains. During the Dissolution of the Monasteries in 1536, the monks left the island and it passed into private hands. In the early 1600s, George Owen noted that there were eight to ten households on the island.

Pirates found the island was a useful retreat during their marauding of the Pembrokeshire coast. There are suggestions that John Paul Jones, a Scottish-American naval commander, moored here regularly to take in water during the American War of Independence (1777–83). One of the bays is named after him, where a sign declares that he arrived to bury treasure. While the British accused him of piracy, the Americans held Jones as a national hero and founder of their navy.

In 1792 Thomas Kynaston bought Caldey and within a few years he built the mansion next to the old priory. His intention was to tap into Caldey's rich limestone, which was widely used as a fertiliser and the basis of mortar and plaster in building. Kynaston opened the large High Cliff Quarry, which went on to produce 20,000 tons of limestone a year.

In 1835, a tragic accident occurred when quarry workers left the island to return to their homes in Tenby. Unfortunately, they ignored warnings about the rough seas. Their boat was overpowered off St Catherine's Island, just five minutes from Tenby, claiming fifteen lives.

Between 1897 and 1906, the island was owned by the Reverend W.D. Bushell, an amateur archaeologist, who began the restoration of buildings.[8] In 1906, he sold the priory to the Benedictine monks. John Coates Carter, a distinguished architect within the Arts and Crafts movement, was commissioned to draw up ambitious plans for a new abbey (Figure 32).

Carter also restored the medieval St Davids Church and designed a post office and cottages in line with Carlyle's vision for the island to become a peaceful intimate community. The original plans were for the present abbey to act as a private boys' school, whose fees would fund the building of a monastery on the north-east headland. However, these plans were abandoned amid mounting debts. Moreover, Carlyle fell out with the Anglican Church and in 1913 his order converted to Catholicism.

In 1929, the abbey was taken over by Cistercians from Belgium. In the early 1950s, they began to sell bunches of lavender to visitors, which marked the beginning of the island's famous perfume industry. Chocolate making followed in the 1980s (although Spanish Cistercian monks were making chocolate in the 1500s) and their own brand of 'Abbot's Kitchen' is now sold all over the world.

In 2000, the council-owned primary school closed due to the prospect of only one child being on the roll for the new term. This brought an end to around 100 years of schooling on the island. The school building, which had formerly been a tearoom, is now a grade-II-listed building.

In 2016, the island's first reported crime made national news when a father from the West Midlands was fined for hitting his 7-year-old son for misbehaving during a tour of the chocolate-making facilities. The island's commercial manager said that in his forty years on the island, it was the first crime that had been brought to court. More recently, the island has been at the centre of a scandal associated with alleged child abuse. One petition in 2021 called for a probe into child abuse allegations, although these relate to historical cases in the 1970s and 1980s.

---

8   His great-granddaughter, Brenda Wright, and her engineer husband shot a rare film of a family outing to the island in 1955 which can be viewed at https://player.bfi.org.uk/free/film/watch-caldey-island-1955-1955-online

GRASSHOLM

Grassholm covers 22 acres and lies 8 miles west of Skomer. Sheep grazed here at various times through to the nineteenth century and fishermen from Marloes would occasionally spend a few nights on the island while fishing for lobsters.

The naturalist Robert Drane visited the island in the 1890s and remarked upon its barren, inhospitable state; yet it felt secure and free. Today, Grassholm is known for its colony of gannets, who took up home following persecution on the island of Lundy where their eggs were stolen. (Widespread cruelty to birds, which included cutting the wings of living birds for use as adornment on women's hats, forced the passing of the Sea Birds Protection Act in 1869.)

Grassholm was the setting of what is possibly the first natural history documentary in the world. Filmed in 1937, with the support of the Royal Navy, the fifteen-minute documentary was entitled *The Private Life of the Gannets*.[9] It was the brainchild of Roger Lockley, Julian Huxley and the acclaimed Hollywood cinematographer, Osmond Borradaile.

In more recent times, studies there have shown how gannets make use of plastics and other flotsam gathered from the sea when building their nests. Unfortunately, some of the chicks get entangled in it as they grow and cannot escape. The RSPB rescues hundreds each year and estimates that there are over 18 tons of plastic on Grassholm.

Removing the plastic will disrupt the gannets and, in any event, they are likely to replace it with more plastic. Short of preventing plastic from entering the sea in the first place, there seems to be no solution to this catch-22. Although the colony is doing well in general, gannets also face the problem of mistaking plastic in the sea for fish. Other environmental problems, such as the dumping of unwanted netting and fishing gear, causes further pain and misery for the gannets and other birdlife.

---

9   It can be viewed at: https://player.bfi.org.uk/free/film/watch-private-life-of-the-gannets-1934-online

RAMSEY

Ramsey Island is located off St Davids Head and is about 2 miles in length. Sophisticated aerial computer surveys have revealed the location of ancient fields, round barrows and a fort dating back more than 4,000 years. This scanning technique is needed in areas which are either inaccessible on foot or are too subtle to see on the ground, due to bracken and scrub vegetation.

Legend has it that St Justinian established a monastic cell on Ramsey. He was later murdered on the island for criticising the monks' lifestyle and his body was thrown into the sea, where it floated to the mainland. Another story suggests that he walked across the water carrying his severed head.

Since medieval times, the island has been owned by the Bishop of St Davids. It is now in the hands of the RSPB and is well known for its choughs, who are attracted to the island because of the dung beetles. Other birds include common buzzards, peregrines, northern wheatears, gulls, auks, Manx shearwaters, razorbills and guillemots. Peregrines were first mentioned in 1171 when Henry II first visited Pembrokeshire, waiting to cross to Ireland. The story goes that the king released one of his goshawks ('Norway hawks') to attack a peregrine but found that the latter was victorious, knocking his larger bird from the sky and landing at the monarch's feet. He was so impressed that he insisted that in future his hawks were procured from Ramsey.

The Normans introduced rabbits on the Pembrokeshire islands from the twelfth century when their fur and meat were something of a luxury. The Bishop of St Davids placed rabbits on Ramsey as a source of income. By the nineteenth century, there were so many rabbits on the island that their skins paid for half of its yearly rent. The records show that between 6,000 and 8,000 rabbits were caught in a season.

Ivor Arnold kept a diary of his time as a farmer on Ramsey in the 1900s. He describes the struggle against rats and rabbits to prevent them from ruining the potato crop. Twice a year rabbits were trapped in huge numbers, which offered a lucrative side business and became more profitable than traditional farming.

Most of the rabbits were sent to the mining valleys of South Wales. By 1946, it was claimed that the export of rabbit meat exceeded that of the county's output of beef, mutton and pork combined. Lockley mentioned that in 1954 the rabbit population was seriously hit by myxomatosis, a disease that was introduced deliberately by farmers who had had enough. A Rabbit Clearance Order was passed, which enabled farmers to control and exterminate rabbits because of the damage they inflicted on crops and woodland.

Ramsey is now recognised as a Site of Special Scientific Interest (SSSI) and the RSPB controls the number of visitors. Among its rare wildlife and plants are one of the UK's smallest spiders (*Clubiona genevensis*), dew moths and the granular bush lichen. Its colony of grey seals is the largest in Wales, with up to 700 pups born on the island each year. Sadly, the storm of 2017 killed 75 per cent of the pups – who were battered against the rocks, struck by debris or abandoned by their mothers who sought to save themselves. In total, there are around 5,000 grey seals around Ramsey. An RSPB warden and assistant are the only human occupants on the island.

ST CATHERINE'S

The island, which lies to the east of Tenby's South Beach (Figure 33), is named after the patron saint of spinners and weavers. The ruins of the chapel dedicated to St Catherine were removed when the fort was built between 1868 and 1870 to defend the Welsh coast from the threat of a French invasion. The only other building on the island was a small church, but this was demolished when the fort was constructed.

In 1907 the War Office sold the fort for £500, and it was eventually transformed by the Windsor-Richards family into a luxury holiday home and furnished with antiques and trophies acquired from their big game safaris. Since 1940, the fort has had several owners and since 2019 has been open to the public for most of the year, subject to the tides, weather and daylight. Recent plans to connect the island to Tenby via a footbridge have been turned down on aesthetic grounds by the Pembrokeshire Coast National Park Authority.

Fig. 33 St Catherine's Island, Tenby, 1853. (*National Library of Wales*)

ST MARGARET'S

This small tidal island is joined to Caldey by a ridge of treacherous rock when the tide is very low. It is not recommended to visit the island, although boat trips from Tenby take visitors around it. A small chapel had been built on the island which was later converted into a house for lime quarry workers. The quarry almost splits the island into two. It is now a nature reserve under the care of the Wildlife Trust and hosts one of the country's largest colony of cormorants, as well as guillemots, razorbills, kittiwakes, shags and various gulls.

SKOKHOLM

Skokholm has been occupied periodically since prehistoric times. In the eighteenth century, a farmhouse and outbuildings were erected. Farming continued in the nineteenth century when James Davies, a farmer from Dale, employed two dairy maids to tend the cows on the island. The butter would be shipped in tubs across to the mainland. Davies drowned in 1861 along with a boy while crossing to the island.

The farm was next rented by Captain Henry Edward Harrison from Waterston, near Milford. Harrison died on the island, and news of his death was communicated to the mainland by the lighting of fires. One of his granddaughters recalled sitting on his coffin as the men rowed back to the mainland.

The island is now owned by the Wildlife Trust of South and West Wales, which limits the number of prearranged visitors so as not to interfere with the tens of thousands of nesting seabirds. It is possible to stay overnight in the island's cottage with rooms offering solar-powered hot water and electric lighting.

SKOMER

Skomer has an area of less than 3km² but is the third-largest island in Wales, after Anglesey, in the north-west. Its Viking name, meaning 'Cleft Island', is named after the island's shape. The rocks known as Jack Sound separate Skomer from the mainland, covering only 600m, although landing is awkward, if not dangerous, because of the high cliffs.

The remains of prehistoric huts, animal enclosures and field boundaries have been found, suggesting a long history of farming on the island. In the 1840s, Skomer was let to Edward Robinson, a London merchant and widower, who moved to the island with his three young children. Robinson, who had studied agriculture, kept a herd of red deer, pheasants, partridges and a flock of Cochin-China fowl. He also followed the custom of shooting many rare birds which were stuffed and mounted in glass cases.

Captain Vaughan Palmer Davies, Robinson's son-in-law, took over the farm lease. Davies was born in Dale and before moving to Skomer, traded in opium as he commanded sailing clippers trading between Bombay, Calcutta and Hong Kong. Davies erected a huge flagstaff (formerly a ship's mast) to communicate with the outside world. The hoisting of one heather bush meant that boat-men were needed, two bushes told them to bring a blacksmith and three meant a doctor was needed.

Davies also rented Skokholm island for the grazing of sheep, ponies and red deer. He kept an eye on their welfare by means of a powerful spyglass. Davies left Skomer in 1892, at the age of 66.

Although farming resumed, it was abandoned again in 1949 due to difficulties in transporting produce and working the land. Over recent years, Skomer has been under the care of the Wildlife Trust of South and West Wales and is one of the most important seabird breeding sites in Europe.

Most visitors arrive to see the puffins when they feed their chicks in June and July. The golden rule is to stay on the paths, to avoid trampling on the burrows that the puffins dig as their nesting sites. Other birds include razorbills, guillemots, choughs, black-backed gulls, peregrine falcons, curlews and the world's largest colony of Manx shearwaters, with over 300,000 breeding pairs.

The rabbit population, originally brought to the island 600 years ago for food and fur, was decimated by 90 per cent follow-ing an outbreak of myxomatosis in 2006. Other wildlife includes the Skomer vole, which is unique to the island.

The old farmhouse provides accommodation for a small team of volunteers and acts as a centre point from which to explore the 4-mile island, which is walkable within three or so hours.

THE HATS AND BARRELS

These rocks were apparently named after their appearance at cer-tain times of the tide. Barrel Rock is the largest, but only extends to 12m. Many shipwrecks have been discovered in this area of treacherous waters and strong tides, which makes it a popular diving site.

22

FAMOUS PEMBROKESHIRE PEOPLE

The following brief biographies, in chronological order, outline a few figures who have proved influential in the history of Pembrokeshire.

ST NON (*c.*6TH CENTURY AD)

Non was the mother of St David, the patron saint of Wales. She was the daughter of Cynir, a local prince. Legend has it that she gave birth alone on the cliffside near Caerfai on 1 March 550, against the background of a thunderstorm. Non, however, was said to have basked in beautiful sunshine during childbirth.

During her labour pains, Non is said to have gripped a stone so hard that her fingerprints were left on it and it split in two. Such legends were crafted to associate Non and David with images of Jesus and the Virgin Mary. Whether they happened in reality did not matter. The 'truth' lay in engaging people's feelings and connecting them to God.

The circumstances of the birth are not uplifting. Despite the fact that Non was a nun, this did not offer the protection that one might think – she was raped by Sant, a prince of Ceredigion.

Several ruins are linked to Non, including a chapel and holy well built on the spot where she gave birth to David. Non has also been commemorated in the wider world – there is a church and holy well dedicated to her in Altarnon, Cornwall, where she settled and she was buried in a church in Dirinon, in Brittany.

The story of a raped nun who survived, despite the likely shunning and shame, could be said to convey a message of hope for women who experience violence and abuse.

ST DAVID (*c.*AD 520–89)

Much of what is known about St David comes from the eleventh-century writings of the hagiographer Rhygyfarch, then Bishop of St Davids. Clearly, there is a need for caution in accepting what he says, given that he lived 500 years after David and his inclination to enhance the saint's importance and the greatness of the city of St Davids ahead of Canterbury. He did so by attributing miracles to David's life, the most famous of which was the story of the ground rising under his feet as he addressed a church congress at Llanddewi Brefi (in Ceredigion) so all could hear him. However, there are generally accepted facts about David:

- He was born on the shore of St Bride's Bay.
- Non named her son *Dewidd* or *Dewi*. David ('beloved') was adopted as a more accessible English form.
- He established a monastery on the spot where St Davids Cathedral now stands.
- David and his monks lived an ascetic life. 'He that does not work, neither shall he eat,' declared David.
- He was a vegetarian and teetotaller called 'the Waterman' – which is ironic, given the tradition of raising a toast to him on St Davids Day.
- David travelled around southern England, Wales and Brittany preaching and founding monasteries. He also visited Jerusalem.
- He eventually returned to *Vallis Rosina* ('Valley of the Roses') to establish a monastery, where St Davids Cathedral now stands.
- Pope Calixtus II canonised David around 1120.
- In 1338, the Archbishop of Canterbury declared that the Festival of St Davids would be held on 1 March.
- His last words to his followers were, 'Be joyful, keep the faith, do the little things you have seen me do'. The phrase

'*Gwnewch y pethau bychain*' ('Do the little things') is well known in Wales.
• David was buried in his own monastery.

David's shrine was destroyed by fire in AD 645 and although rebuilt was subject to further assault at the hands of the Vikings. The latest restoration occurred in 2012 and the shrine continues to attract pilgrims. There are over fifty churches dedicated to David, along with hundreds of St Davids societies around the world, which celebrates, preserves and promotes Welsh culture.

GERALD OF WALES (*c.*1146–1223)

Born in Manorbier Castle around 1146, Gerald of Wales was one of the most fascinating figures in the Middle Ages. As the biographer Robert Bartlett points out, Gerald served many roles – scholar, churchman, agent of English kings, diplomat, courtier, propagandist, reformer, champion of the Welsh church and would-be Crusader.

Gerald was of mixed descent. His father, William de Barri, came from Norman settlers who took their name from Barry Island, while his mother, Angharad, was the daughter of Nest and granddaughter of Rhys ap Tewdwr. His father and uncle, David FitzGerald, who was Bishop of St Davids, encouraged Gerald to follow a career in the Church. Gerald records that as a child playing on the beach, he made churches of sand while his brother made sandcastles. He was determined to serve God and attain high office in the Church.

While he was from a privileged background, Gerald needed to display considerable resilience and persistence. At school, he was ridiculed by his teachers, who called him 'thick, thicker, thickest!' and 'silly, sillier and silliest!' Following his monastic education at Gloucester, he attended the University of Paris, the best in Europe, where he spent ten years studying during the first of two lengthy visits. He returned to England and Wales around the age of 30 and was appointed personal legate to the Archbishop of Canterbury.

Gerald was zealous to reform the Church and was empowered to sanction those who stepped out of line, including excommunicating the Sheriff of Pembrokeshire, who had taken eight oxen from Pembroke Priory, and sacking the elderly Archdeacon of Brecon for living with his mistress. Gerald's uncle David was appointed as his replacement, a post he held for many years.

In 1876, following the death of his uncle, Gerald eyed the prospect of succeeding him as the new Bishop of St Davids. Instead, King Henry chose Peter de Leia, an Anglo-Norman by birth, and a crestfallen Gerald returned to Paris to resume his studies for a second stint.

Gerald was proud of his Norman-Welsh lineage although it was something of a mixed blessing. The Welsh regarded Gerald as too Norman and the Normans considered him too Welsh. And yet Gerald was ideally placed for negotiating on behalf of the king with Welsh princes and Norman barons. As one historian put it, Gerald 'was gossipy but very shrewd'. Hence, he became an asset at the royal court, working as chaplain, clerk and adviser – but this was not his dream.

The bishopric was nearly within Gerald's grasp when, on 22 June 1199, he was unanimously elected Bishop of St Davids. However, this needed to be approved by the Crown and the Pope. Gerald made three separate journeys to Rome, lobbying for papal support, encountering bandits, snowy Alpine passes and even a kidnapping, but to no avail. His enemies within the Church, led by Archbishop of Canterbury Hubert Walter, ensured that Gerald's efforts were in vain. Their fear was that David might lead an independent church, an archbishopric, undermining Canterbury.

By the age of 60, Gerald had finally given up hopes of achieving his dream with the appointment of a new Bishop of St Davids, which he accepted with good grace, announcing, 'I have struggled enough'. He lived for a further twenty years.

Gerald's personality was clearly one of his assets. Archbishop Baldwin remarked that he had never seen so many tears in his life when watching the audience's emotional response to Gerald's preaching at Haverfordwest. What made this even more remarkable was the fact that the audience were Welsh or English speakers, who could not have understood a word that Gerald said in Norman-French and Latin, the language of the Church. More than 200 were said to have leapt forward to take their Crusading vows. As it turned out, there is little evidence that many recruits ended up fighting in Jerusalem, but this should not detract from the story of Gerald's efforts.

Gerald had a way with words, combining history, ethnography and topography. He wrote at least seventeen books, every word was written in Latin. The most famous is his diary-style *Journey Through Wales* (1191), as he toured the land along with Archbishop Baldwin in their efforts to recruit for the Third Crusade. This was followed by *Description of Wales* in 1194. In this, he recorded what he saw on his travels, including descriptions of wildlife, such as the last beaver on the River Teifi. He did tend to embellish his commentary and included factual errors, for example, suggesting that beavers castrate themselves to avoid danger.

He died around 1223 and is buried in St Davids Cathedral. According to Culturenet Cymru, Gerald has been described as the most influential writer in defining Wales to the outside world. Many of his general comments about the people and country and could be said to remain true nearly 900 years later.

NEST (1085–*c*.1136)

Nest was described by Edward Laws as 'almost the only Welsh woman who has inscribed her name on the pages of history'. She certainly led an eventful life, bearing at least nine children to five different men.

Nest was the daughter of Rhys ap Tewdwr, King of Deheubarth. He had established peaceful terms with William the Conqueror but when the Norman king died in 1087, this changed. William Rufus, the new king, pursued a more militant policy and Rhys was killed in a battle at Brecon. The 14-year-old Nest was taken hostage to the king's court where she and the future King Henry I, William's brother and successor, became lovers. Nest gave birth to his son, Henry FitzHenry, in 1103.

The womanising King Henry, who fathered at least twenty-eight illegitimate children by numerous mistresses, married Nest off to one of his barons, Gerald de Windsor, who was Constable of Pembroke Castle and ruler of her father's former lands. Gerald built new castles at Carew and Cilgerran to strengthen his position against the Welsh although, given Nest's Welsh lineage, relations with the Welsh princes were cordial enough. Gerald and Nest were the grandparents of Giraldus Cambrensis.

Owain, Nest's second cousin and son of the Welsh royal household of Powys, attended a Christmas banquet held at Cilgerran Castle in 1109, hosted by Gerald and Nest. Owain was overcome by her beauty, likened to the fabled Helen of Troy, and boldly decided to abduct her. His men started a fire as a distraction and mounted an attack, which led Gerald to escape down a privy chute, while Nest and two of her sons were taken prisoner by Owain. The castle was then plundered.

It is unclear whether Nest willingly entered into relations with Owain or was raped, but the upshot was that his actions triggered a minor civil war when Owain's enemies were encouraged by King Henry to take up arms against the kingdom of Powys. Owain and his father fled to Ireland and Nest reunited with her husband.

When Owain later returned, under the impression that the king needed his services to defeat other Welsh rebels, he was ambushed by Gerald and killed by Flemish archers.

When Gerald died, Nest soon entered another relationship, marrying Stephen, the Constable of Cardigan and she bore him two sons.

This is an exciting story compiled by the Welsh chroniclers, who were keen to enhance the warrior status of Owain and present the Normans in a less favourable light. Nest may have had ten children with five different fathers, but whether this denotes a woman of considerable political shrewdness in capitalising on her beauty and family connections or reflects a story of abuse and abduction among powerful men of the day is debatable.

Nest's many descendants were key influences in the story of Pembrokeshire, including her grandson, Gerald of Wales, who was silent on her promiscuity. Genealogists have suggested that Nest is related to both the Tudor and Stuart monarchs, as well as Diana, Princess of Wales and John F. Kennedy, President of the United States!

GEORGE OWEN (1552–1613)

George Owen was born in the parish of Nevern, the son of a successful lawyer. Owen also trained in London to become a lawyer himself, but his interests turned to antiquities and his love of Pembrokeshire. He is buried in Nevern, where he is commemorated as the 'Patriarch of English Geologists'.

His most famous work is *Description of Pembrokeshire*, which appeared in 1603. It offers plenty of wonderful information on history, wildlife, folklore, landscape and other subjects. He introduced the phrase 'Little England beyond Wales' to describe south Pembrokeshire, which was derived from his observation of how English was used, the prevalence of English surnames, building styles, diet and village placenames.

It is less well known that Owen started a second book with the aim of detailing the history of every parish in the county. We do not know whether he completed this and it is even thought that Owen may have written a third manuscript, mentioned by an antiquary in 1717, but this has not surfaced. Sadly, we also have no surviving portrait of Owen, assuming that one was painted, as it was very much the fashion among the Elizabethan gentry. Surprisingly, neither are there any written records of what he looked like and he kept no diaries.

SIR JOHN PERROT (1528–92)

Born in the family home of Haroldston Manor near Haverfordwest, John Perrot became a major advisor to Queen Elizabeth I. He was rumoured to be the illegitimate son of Henry VIII. His mother, Mary Berkeley, was a lady at the royal court. He went on to serve forty years in high political office. He held many titles and was MP for Pembrokeshire constituencies twice, but despite his high profile, as historian Roger Turvey points out, the lack of a private diary and limited personal correspondence makes it difficult for historians to understand the motives for some of his actions.

Perrot was given the task of defeating the Irish and colonising their lands. In one infamous episode, he ordered the heads of fifty deceased rebels to be cut off and fixed to the market cross at Killmallock. Perrot was awarded Carew Castle for his work in Ireland. He was later accused of treason, although Elizabeth refused to sign the death warrant. Nonetheless, he was imprisoned in the Tower of London, where he died in 1592, possibly from poisoning.

ROBERT RECORDE (1510–58)

The Welsh Tourist Board once ran a campaign in which it claimed that Wales invented equality. It was referring to Robert Recorde (Figure 34), the Tenby-born mathematician, who was the first to use the equals sign in mathematical operations 'to avoid the tedious repetition of equals to'. It appeared in 1557 in his work *The Whetstone of Witte* (a digital copy can be viewed on the National Library of Wales website).

Recorde was also physician to both Edward VI and Mary I and served as Controller of the Royal Mint. Unfortunately, he ran into financial difficulties and was imprisoned for debt. He died in Southwark Gaol at the age of just 46.

Fig. 34 Robert Recorde (*Wellcome Trust, Attribution 4.0 International. (CC BY 4.0)*)

JOHN ROBERTS (1682–1722)

John Roberts was born in Casnewydd Bach, near Puncheston, where there is a memorial stone. For some unknown reason, he changed his name from John to Bartholomew. Pirates often adopted aliases and it is possible that he was inspired by a well-known buccaneer, Bartholomew Sharp.

Buccaneers operated within the Caribbean and the Pacific coast of Central America. Roberts went to sea at the age of 13 and by 1719 was serving as second mate on the slave ship, *Princess*. This was anchored off the Gold Coast (now Ghana) town of Anomabu, where it was attacked by pirates led by another Pembrokeshire man, Howell Davis from Milford Haven. Roberts and other crew members were forced to join the pirates.

According to Charles Johnson's history of piracy, written in 1724, Roberts was at first not keen on becoming a pirate but changed his mind at the lure of commanding his own ship. Roberts

Fig. 35 Barti Ddu. (*Johnson, c.1724*)

soon demonstrated his navigational skills and Davis liked the fact that he could share secrets by speaking Welsh to Roberts. When Davis was killed by the Portuguese in an attack that went wrong, Roberts was elected as the new captain of the *Royal Rover*.

During his brief time as a pirate, he captured over 400 ships and amassed a fortune. Among his prized captures were 40,000 gold coins and jewellery designed for the King of Portugal, seized from the *Sagrada Familia*, despite it having forty guns and a crew of 170.

Roberts always wore a red coat, waistcoat and breeches whenever he went into battle and was one of the first to fly the Jolly Roger, the traditional pirate flag. His motto was 'A short life and a merry one' and he earned a reputation as a violent and bloodthirsty criminal, leaving sea captains fearful of sailing in open waters. However, as a teetotaller, he departed from the conventional depiction of drunken pirates.

Eventually, two Royal Navy ships traced Roberts to the African coast, where he was eventually shot in the throat and more than fifty of his crew were hanged for piracy. After his death, Roberts was known as '*Barti Ddu*' (Figure 35). Roberts has been widely depicted in popular culture, from video games to novels, television programmes and films. The passage of time renders a pirate such as Roberts something of a cult hero, with historical accuracy being of less importance than a good story.

SIR THOMAS PICTON (1758–1815)

General Sir Thomas Picton of Poyston has long been admired for his patriotism and military zeal. He was thanked in Parliament on seven separate occasions and was popular among the general public and his men, retiring with honours to Ferryside (in Carmarthenshire). The writer Trevor Breverton ranks Picton in the Top 100 Great Welshmen, celebrating his forty-five years as a soldier, but overlooks the darker aspects of his career.

Picton was also a ruthless imperialist, the 'Tyrant of Trinidad', whose cruelty as its first governor came to the fore in 1803. He authorised the torture of Louisa Calderon, a free 14-year-old girl who had been accused of theft. She was hung from a scaffold by her wrist for an hour, her body weight supported on an upturned wooden peg, not sharp enough to piece the skin but a cause of unbearable pain. Picton was found guilty and convicted of torturing, decapitating and burning alive slaves accused of sorcery, witchcraft and necromancy. Louisa Calderon was brought to London to offer evidence.

The prosecution case was led by the notable reforming lawyer William Garrow and although Picton was convicted, the verdict was later overturned on the grounds that Trinidad at the time was under Spanish law, which sanctioned torture.

In the light of this, Haverfordwest Civic Society's blue plaque guide makes for uneasy reading, 'Picton's place in history was assured by his incredible bravery after he returned to active service as a general in the Napoleonic Wars'. It describes his skill and gallantry in storming the castle of Badajoz and his famous words, 'If we cannot win the castle let us die upon its walls', which were said to inspire the troops.

Picton was the highest-ranking British officer to fall at the Battle of Waterloo on 18 June 1815. The Duke of Wellington described him as 'a rough foul-mouthed devil, but very capable'.

Picton has been commemorated in local place names and roads in Milford Haven, Tenby and Neyland, pubs, monuments and even towns in New Zealand, Canada and Australia. In 1978, Haverfordwest's new comprehensive school was renamed Sir Thomas Picton School (it closed as part of a merger in 2018).

In 2020, a sign of changing values was demonstrated following the Black Lives Matter protests when Cardiff City Council ordered the covering up of Picton's statue in a 'Welsh Heroes' gallery in the City Hall. The blue plaque in Haverfordwest was also removed in 2020 by the building's owner, who was fearful that it might be attacked.

DAVID SALMON (1852–1944)

David Salmon was born in Newport and became one of Wales's leading educationalists. Having served as a teacher's apprentice or pupil-teacher in Haverfordwest, Salmon completed his teacher training in London and then stayed on as a tutor at the Borough Road College. He then became headmaster of a London board school, before returning to Wales in 1891 to take up the position of principal of Swansea Training College for Women, a post he held for thirty years until his retirement in 1922. He wrote more than thirty publications, mostly school textbooks and academic papers, covering topics such as the Quakers in Pembrokeshire and the French (Fishguard) Invasion of 1797.

GWEN JOHN (1876–1939)

Gwen John was born in Haverfordwest and raised as a child in Tenby, where she started to paint. She followed her younger brother Augustus to study art in London in 1896. She never returned to Wales, moving to Paris to study under Whistler and model for Rodin, with whom she had an affair for many years.

Her work is characterised by simple, restrained brushwork in contrast to her brother's flamboyant, large paintings. The subjects varied from portraits of nuns to cats and household interiors. She adopted a style known as 'intimism', in which a single figure dominates the composition. Her brother regarded Gwen as the greatest female painter of her age. Although she never stopped painting, she struggled to make a commercial success of her work.

AUGUSTUS JOHN (1878–1961)

Augustus John established an international reputation as a leading portrait painter with subjects including Thomas Hardy, George Bernard Shaw, Dylan Thomas, and T.E. Lawrence. In 1937, he was invited to paint the Queen Mother (at the time, the reigning monarch). He responded by saying that he would stay in a pub near Windsor Castle and she could visit him secretly for sittings. She refused.

The incident reflects his reputation as a Bohemian artist with his red beard and outlandish dress. He drank heavily and lived a promiscuous, nomadic life, often camping with gypsies. He fathered many children, including illegitimate ones who were known as 'demi-Johns'. Trevor Breverton cites the story that whenever John walked down Chelsea's King's Road, he used to pat the heads of all the children, just in case one was his son or daughter.

As to the quality of his artwork, critics claimed he took easy money by painting the rich and famous, although his expensive lifestyle and large family may have given him little option. John's early Post-Impressionist drawings are regarded as his best work. Both Augustus and his sister are honoured in Tenby Art Gallery and Museum.

WALDO WILLIAMS (1904–71)

Former Bishop of St Davids, Rowan Williams regarded Waldo Williams as probably Wales's greatest twentieth-century poet. Waldo was born in Haverfordwest and when he was 7, the family moved to Mynachlog-ddu, where he learnt Welsh. He attended Narberth Grammar School and then the University of Wales, Aberystwyth, before returning to Pembrokeshire as a primary school teacher.

Teaching was very much a family affair. His father, Edwal Williams, was a gifted teacher and former headmaster at Haverfordwest, while his sister Mary also taught in Fishguard Grammar School.

Both his parents were Christian pacifists and he opposed the Second World War on the basis that all men were brothers under God's sovereignty. He married in 1941 but his wife, Linda, died in 1943.

Williams took up teaching jobs in England but retained a deep connection with Wales and the Welsh language, which is reflected in his poetry and his convictions. In 1936, he wrote a collection of children's verses called *Cerddi'r Plant*, which was well received. He only published one volume of poems, *Dail Pren* ('Leaves of a Tree').

Williams opposed plans in 1947 to transform the Preseli Hills into a permanent military training base, describing the War Office as '*y bwystfil*' ('the beast'). Local historian Hefin Wyn highlights the successful efforts of the Precelly Preservation Committee, supported by Williams, in safeguarding the 'sacred' heritage of the Preseli Hills which supplied the bluestones for Stonehenge.

Waldo returned to Pembrokeshire in 1950 and became the county's first Plaid Cymru candidate in 1959. He opposed national conscription and the paying of taxes to support this. Hence, he was imprisoned for two six-week periods and his property claimed in lieu of tax. The Quaker Friends at Milford Haven stepped in and redeemed his home, and Waldo became a Quaker, whose beliefs aligned with his pacifist views.

Waldo was a well-known figure in Haverfordwest. He was often seen on his bicycle, wearing his distinctive yellow cape, or walking around the town. It was here that he planned to retire but he was struck with illness and died in St Thomas Hospital. He is laid to rest in Blaenconin Chapel burial ground in Llandissilio.

23

FOLKTALES AND CUSTOMS

Pembrokeshire is rich in folklore and folk customs. 'Folklore' describes the tales, beliefs, myths, songs, riddles and proverbs that have been passed down by word of mouth from one generation to another. 'Folk customs' have a broader remit and include activities such as dance and craftwork. To illustrate, Trefor Owen points out that the folk custom is the act of singing rather than the music itself, which is a form of folklore.

The county has long been regarded as the 'land of mystery' or the Enchanted Land (*Gwlad yr Hud*). The *Mabinogi* includes various legends and myths, such as the boar Twrch Twyth slaying several of King Arthur's men and turning them into stone near Cerrigmarchogion. The village of Brynberian suffered at the hands of the nasty giant Afanc, while the huge boulders known as Carnedd Meibion Owen are said to be the legacy of an inheritance squabble between three brothers, who were also giants.

In tight-knit communities, folklore and folk customs played a key social role. They brought people together and were particularly associated with commemorating births, deaths, courtships and marriages, as well as the passing of the seasons and festivals such as harvest, Easter and Christmas. Some of these customs were rooted in pagan beliefs. For example, in 1910 the *Pembroke County Guardian* reported that the drawing of chalk lines around Pembrokeshire doorsteps was designed to keep out evil spirits and dated back to the ancient Druids.

Christmas attracted many customs. In north Pembrokeshire, in the middle of the nineteenth century, 25 December was the first day of a three-week holiday during which farm work was suspended. To symbolise this, the plough was carried into the home and placed under the table in the room where the meals were eaten. Some farmers then wetted the plough with beer before drinking it, to signify that while the plough was suspended, it would be returned to after the holiday.

Families stayed up overnight or rose early in the morning to attend the *Plygain* service at the parish church. The word '*plygain*' derives from the Latin '*pulli*' ('young cockerel') and '*cantus*' ('song'), and by implication the return of light or daybreak. The service times varied between 3 a.m. and 6 a.m.

On Christmas Eve, young people gathered at different farmhouses around a large fire to enjoy a night of merriment with eating and drinking interspersed with singing until the sound of the church bell was heard. Inevitably, the raucous behaviour did not align well with the traditional church atmosphere and might explain why the custom declined, as this newspaper article suggested in 1879:

> It is scarcely necessary to say that a dimly lighted church filled by a congregation made up of parties of young people who have spent the night in uproarious mirth is not as quiet as a church should be when religious services are held.

The newspaper article blamed the *Plygain* for damaging the reverential reputation of the Welsh among visitors. In Nonconformist chapels, the singing of carols was soon abandoned because of the disorderly nature.

In Tenby, crowds ushered in Christmas by carrying torches, shouting verses and blowing cow horns before escorting the rector from his house to the church. In the outlying villages, residents brought their own candles because there was rarely any provision in the church for lighting at night-time.

Certain customs alarmed the authorities. The folklorist Trevor Owen cites the example of 'Holly-beating' on Boxing Day, which involved men and boys armed with large bushes of prickly holly hitting 'the naked and unprotected arms of female domestics and others of a like class' until their arms bled. This was banned in Tenby in 1857 but continued elsewhere in Wales.

At Marloes, on Twelfth Night (6 January), the villagers hunted wrens and killed one to mark the death of winter. The poor bird was then placed in an ornamental box dressed in ribbons and carried around the village. Such a relic from 1869 can be seen in St Fagan's National Museum of History.

Bringing in the New Year was a time of revelry rather than reflection. It was common for crowds of boys to visit neighbours' houses at three or four o'clock in the early morning, carrying vessels of cold spring water freshly drawn from the well that morning, along with a twig of holly, myrtle or another evergreen. The boys would sprinkle the water over the hands and faces of those they visited and every room they entered, in return for the payment of a few pence. If they were not allowed entry, water would be sprinkled on the door frames.

Another popular tradition was *Calennig* ('New Year celebrations'), involved the giving of gifts. Children typically went from house to house conveying good wishes for people's health and prosperity for the year ahead and carrying fruit such as an apple or orange stuck full of corn and sometimes decorated with a sprig of evergreen.

On 13 January, the inhabitants of Cwm Gwaun near Fishguard prepare for the New Year according to the old Julian calendar which dated back to Julius Caesar and Roman days. In 1752, their ancestors refused to adopt the new Gregorian calendar that had been introduced by Pope Gregory, even though this more accurately reflected the actual time it takes the Earth to circle once around the Sun. Their resistance was partly because the changes were felt to be Catholic, and in making September shorter, people felt as if eleven days were being unjustly taken away from them.

Equally popular was the *Mari Lwyd* ('grey Mary'), called *Y Gynfasfarch* ('The Canvas Horse') in Pembrokeshire. This involved decorating a horse's skull with colourful ribbons and a white sheet. This was then carried around the neighbourhood to celebrate that the darkest days of the year were over and spring was pending, encouraging householders to arise from their winter sleep.

In recent years, the National Museum of Wales and organisations such as *Mentrau Iaith* have raised awareness of these ancient traditions through exhibitions and re-enactments.

24

PEMBROKESHIRE PUBS AND INNS

Pembrokeshire has a wonderful range of pubs. In 2021, the Dyffryn Arms in Cwm Gwaun, for example, was voted the UK's best 'pub walk', where walkers can rest with a decent pint and food in front of a roaring fire. Keith Johnson, who was born in a pub, has catalogued the pubs of Pembrokeshire. The following are among his favourites. I have updated the notes below each entry.

THE GRIFFIN, DALE

An award-winning pub renowned for its locally supplied seafood.

CRESSELLY ARMS, KILGETTY

This traditional riverside pub overlooks the Cleddau Estuary, although some reviews (as of 2023) on TripAdvisor are decidedly mixed!

THE OLD POINT HOUSE, ANGLE

This grade-II-listed farmhouse pub overlooks Angle Bay. Its maritime history decorates the walls. The pub closed in 2020, but has since reopened under new owners.

THE STACKPOLE INN, STACKPOLE

Over the last decade or so, the inn has won many awards for its food, drink and hospitality. It serves Welsh beers, including Double Dragon and the Reverend James.

HOPE AND ANCHOR, TENBY

Dating from the 1800s, the pub has been a traditional gathering place for fishermen to celebrate their catches and is now popular with locals and tourists alike.

TAFARN SINC, ROSEBUSH

The 'Zinc Pub' was originally built as a hotel in the 1870s to attract visitors to the village as a health resort. It is now a community-owned enterprise. It is also connected to the Maenclochog Railway and has the station platform in its grounds.

THE SLOOP, PORTHGAIN

Built in 1743 to quench the thirst of local slate workers, the renovated pub offers seasonal Welsh dishes and specials.

TEIFI NETPOOL INN, ST DOGMAELS

Originally built in the 1600s, but fully refurbished, the Netpool in the name refers to the netting of salmon in a pool of the river below the pub. This heritage is reflected in the pub décor.

NAG'S HEAD, ABERCYCH

The pub is in the peaceful Cych Valley and has a reputation for local real ales, fine wine and seasonal food.

THE FISHGUARD ARMS, FISHGUARD

A small and vibrant terraced pub which features a 1930s bar counter, wood-panelled walls and log fire, and where ale is served from casks.

USEFUL WEBSITES

The official Pembrokeshire Tourism website:
https://www.visitpembrokeshire.com

A website associated with Brian John's novels set in
'Martha Morgan Country', named after the heroine:
http://www.marthamorgan.co.uk

History of Pembroke Dock maintained by volunteers:
http://www.pembrokedockhistory.co.uk

Mark Muller's website includes various articles on
Pembrokeshire: http://www.mmuller.co.uk

The National Library of Wales website hosts the invaluable
Welsh Newspapers Online: https://www.library.wales

The website of the Pembrokeshire Coast National Park includes
news, education programmes and events:
https://www.pembrokeshirecoast.wales

Pembrokeshire Historical Society website includes lecture programmes, news and publications:
http://www.pembrokeshirehistoricalsociety.co.uk

St Davids Cathedral website maintained by the cathedral team:
https://www.stdavidscathedral.org.uk

The Wildlife Trust of South and West Wales provides information
on its nature reserves, including Skomer and Skokholm Islands:
https://www.welshwildlife.org

History of Crymych website:
http://www.crymych.org.uk/english/hanes.htm

SELECT BIBLIOGRAPHY

BIBLIOGRAPHICAL NOTE

For those who are keenly interested in the history of the county, the most comprehensive reference is the five-volume series produced by the Pembrokeshire Local Historical Society. There is also a broad selection of books on the history and topography of the county's towns, villages and islands. Those produced by Roscoe Howells, Dillwyn Miles, Brian John, and Phil Carradice offer a good starting point.

There are many evocative picture books, although none surpass Simon Hancock's 650-page tome on Victorian and Edwardian Haverfordwest. His experience as curator of the town museum informs an insightful commentary on all aspects of life in Pembrokeshire.

The best architectural study is the Pevsner guide, compiled by Thomas Lloyd, Julian Orbach and Robert Scourfield.

There are lots of publications on the Pembrokeshire National Park and the coastal path. On the latter, my favourite is written by Dennis and Jan Kelsall, who draw on their extensive walking experience to offer a step-by-step guide (almost literally) to walking the 180 miles in fourteen stages.

Bartlett, R., *Gerald of Wales. A Voice of the Middle Ages* (London: Tempus, 2006).

Bennett, T., *Maritime History of Newport Pembrokeshire* (Great Britain: Amazon Books, 2019).

Breverton, T., *100 Great Welshmen* (St Athan: Wales Books, 2001).

Brown, J., *The History of Haverfordwest* (Haverfordwest: L. Brigstocke, 1914).

Carradice, P., *The History of Pembroke Dock* (Pembroke: Accent Press, 2006).

Connop Price, M.R., *Pembrokeshire: The Forgotten Coalfield* (Ashbourne: Landmark, 2004).

Cunliffe, B., *The Ancient Celts* (Oxford: Oxford University Press, 2018).

Curtis, T., *Real South Pembrokeshire* (Bridgend: Seren, 2011).

Davies, G., *Light in the Land: Christianity in Wales 200–2000* (Bridgend: Bryntirion Press, 2002).

Davies, G., *Pembrokeshire Villages* (Sigma Leisure, 2013).

Davies, J., *A History of Wales* (London: Penguin, 2007).

Davies, R., *People, Places, and Passions* (Cardiff: University of Wales Press, 2015).

Driver, T., *Pembrokeshire: Historic Landscapes from the Air* (Aberystwyth: Royal Commission on Ancient Historical Monuments in Wales, 2007).

Evans, W., *St Davids Cathedral* (London: Pitkin, 2002).

Falk, S., *The Light Ages: A Medieval Journey of Discovery* (London: Penguin, 2021).

Fenton, R., *A Historical Tour Through Pembrokeshire* (London: Longman, Hurst, Rees, Orme & Company, 1811).

Fletcher, C., and R. Kipling, *A History of England* (Clarendon Press, Oxford, 1911).

Graeber, D., and D. Wengrow, *The Dawn of Everything: A New History of Humanity* (London: Allen Lane, 2021).

Goodman, R., *How to be a Victorian* (London: Penguin, 2013).

Gosse, P., *Tenby: A Sea-side Holiday* (London: John van Voorst, 1856).

Hancock, S., *A Photographic History of Victorian and Edwardian Haverfordwest* (Haverfordwest: Haverfordwest Town Museum, 2010).

Howell, D.W. (ed.), *An Historical Atlas of Pembrokeshire* (Haverfordwest; Pembrokeshire County History Trust, 2019).

Howells, R., *Caldey Island* (Llandysul: Gomer Press, 1984).

Howells, R., *Old Saundersfoot. From Monkstone to Marros* (Llandysul: Gomer, 1984).

Howells, R., *Pembrokeshire's Islands* (Llandysul: Gomer, 1994).

James, H., 'Roman Pembrokeshire AD 75–150', in James, H., Johnson, M., Murphy, K., and G. Wainwright (eds), *Prehistoric, Roman and Early Medieval Pembrokeshire* (Haverfordwest: Pembrokeshire County History Trust, 2016), pp. 296–339.

Jenkins, J.G., *Pembrokeshire: Its Present and its Past Explored* (Gwasg Carreg Gwalch, 2016).

Kelsall, D. and J., *Walking the Pembrokeshire Coast Path* (Kendal: Cicerone, 2016).

Laws, E., *The History of Little England Beyond Wales, and the Non-Kymric Colony Settled in Pembrokeshire* (1888).

Lewis, S., *A Topographical Dictionary of Wales*, Vol. II (London: S. Lewis & Co, 1833).

Lloyd, H., *The Gentry of South-West Wales, 1540–1640* (Cardiff: University of Wales Press, 1968).

Lloyd, T., Orbach, J., and R. Scourfield, *The Buildings of Wales: Pembrokeshire* (New Haven, Yale University Press, 2004).

Lockley, R., *Pembrokeshire* (London: Hale, 1957).

Malkin, B., *The Scenery, Antiquities, and Biography of South Wales: From Materials Collected During Two Excursions in the Year 1803* (London: Longman & Rees, 1804).

Miles, D., *The Ancient Borough of Newport in Pembrokeshire* (Haverfordwest, 1995).

Miles, D. (ed.), *A History of Haverfordwest* (Llandysul: Gomer, 1999).

Morris, J., *Wales* (London: Viking, 1998).

Mortimer, I., *Human Race: 10 Centuries of Change on Earth* (London: Vintage, 2015).

Morton, H., *In Search of Wales* (London: Methuen, 1932).

Owen, G., *The Description of Pembrokeshire* (Llandysul: Gomer Press, 1994).

Owen, T., *Welsh Folk Customs* (Cardiff: University of Wales Press, 1964).

Phillips, L., *Pembroke Dockyard and the Old Navy: A Bicentennial History* (Stroud: The History Press, 2014).

Pryor, F., *Britain BC: Life in Britain and Ireland Before the Roman*s (London: Harper Perennial, 2004).

Rees, T., *Topographical and Historical Description of South Wales* (London: London: Sherwood, Neely, and Jones,1820).

Rees, V., *The Shell Guide to South-West Wales: Pembrokeshire and Carmarthenshire* (London: Shell, 1963).

Richards, B., *Pembrokeshire Under Fire* (Pembroke Dock: Paterchurch Publications, 1983).

Robinson, T., *The Worst Jobs in History* (London: Pan Macmillan, 2004).

Simond, L., *Journal of a Tour and Residence in Great Britain During the Years 1810 and 1811 By a French Traveller* (Edinburgh: George Ramsay and Company, 1815).

The Benedictines of Caldey Island (Isle of Caldey: The Abbey, 1907).

Thomas, M., and J. Warren (eds), *Haverfordwest Plaque Trail* (Haverfordwest: Haverfordwest Civic Society, 1999).

Thornhill-Timmins, H., *Nooks and Corners of Pembrokeshire* (London: Elliot Stock, 1895).

Turvey, R., 'Sir John Perrot, Henry VIII's bastard? The Destruction of a Myth' in *Transactions of the Honourable Society of Cymmrodorion* (1992) pp. 79–94.

Turvey, R., *Pembrokeshire: the Concise History* (Cardiff: University of Wales Press, 2005).

Winder, R., *Bloody Foreigners* (London: Abacus, 2004).

INDEX